Paddling Everglades National Park

A Guide to the Best Paddling Adventures

Loretta Lynn Leda

FALCONGUIDES

GUILFORD, CONNECTICUT
HELENA, MONTANA
AN IMPRINT OF GLOBE PEQUOT PRESS

To my mom, Janice Terese Matyasik, in her memory, for her unending love and belief in me, for her support and encouragement. Even though you may not have been with me physically on these trips, you are always with me in spirit in my journey through life. I will miss coming home from my adventures and sharing my tales and photos of my trips, both domestically and abroad. We never had the opportunity to go to the spa together as we spoke about, so I will take my daughter in your place and think of you. And to another one of my heroes whom I've aways looked up to, my brother Tim Vaughn (SGT MJR US Army). Thank you for all you've done and for your bravery and patriotism to our country. With love and faith.

Thank you!

I love and miss you!

To buy books in quantity for corporate use or incentives, call **(800) 962-0973** or e-mail **premiums@GlobePequot.com**.

FALCONGUIDES®

Copyright © 2010 by Morris Book Publishing, LLC

ALL RIGHTS RESERVED. No part of this book may be reproduced or transmitted in any form by any means, electronic or mechanical, including photocopying and recording, or by any information storage and retrieval system, except as may be expressly permitted in writing from the publisher. Requests for permission should be addressed to Globe Pequot Press, Attn: Rights and Permissions Department, P.O. Box 480, Guilford, CT 06437.

Falcon, FalconGuides, and Outfit Your Mind are registered trademarks of Morris Book Publishing, LLC.

Interior photos by Loretta Lynn Leda

Project editor: David Legere
Maps by Bruce Grubbs © Morris Book Publishing, LLC

Library of Congress Cataloging-in-Publication Data is available on file.

ISBN: 978-0-7627-1149-9

Printed in the United States of America

10 9 8 7 6 5 4 3 2 1

The author and Globe Pequot Press assume no liability for accidents happening to, or injuries sustained by, readers who engage in the activities described in this book.

Contents

Acknowledgments viii
Introduction 1
Paddling Equipment 11
Safety 13
Camping and Launch Sites...14

Paddle Routes

Collier-Seminole State Park
1. Blackwater River Trail...20

Port of the Islands
2. Faka Union River Route 26

The Western Everglades
3. East River Canoe Route (Fakahatchee Strand State Preserve) 30
4. Turner River (Big Cypress National Preserve and Everglades National Park) ...34
5. Halfway Creek 37
6. Halfway Creek to Barron Lakes Loop..41
7. Barron River, West Fork 44

Chokoloskee Island and Everglades City
8. Barron River, East Fork..50
9. Barron River to Seagrape Drive Ramp..52

Ten Thousand Islands
10. Sandfly Island...56
11. Gopher Creek 59
12. Indian Key Pass to Picnic Key..62
13. Tiger Key 65
14. Picnic Key..69
15. Jewell Key 72
16. Rabbit Key 75
17. Last Huston Bay Route 78
18. A Scenic Mangrove Tunnel on the Wilderness Waterway 80
19. Chatham River Route 83
20. Darwin's Place..87

Cape Sable, Whitewater Bay, and Flamingo
21. Big Sable Route 92

22. Nine Mile Pond Loop 94
23. Noble Hammock 97
24. Hells Bay Paddle Trail 98
25. Buttonwood Canal Route 100
26. Bear Lake Canal/Paddle Trail (in the Backcountry) 101
27. Mud Lake Loop 103
28. Whitewater Bay Route 105
29. Labyrinth Route 108
30. Cormorant Pass 110
31. Lane River Route 112
32. North River Route 115
33. The Cutoff Route 118
34. Roberts River Route 121
35. East River Route 123
36. Joe River Route 125
37. Middle Cape Route 127
38. Broad River Route 130
39. Shark Cutoff Route 133

Florida Bay
40. West Lake to Alligator Creek 138
41. Snake Bight Route 140
42. Florida Bay Loop 143
43. Carl Ross Key to Little Rabbit Key (via Man of War Key) 145
44. Little Rabbit Key to Flamingo 147
45. Flamingo to Little Rabbit Key 149
46. The Wilderness Waterway 151
47. Sawgrass Route to Flamingo 155

Honorable Mentions
48. Shingle Creek to Lake Okeechobee 158

Appendix A: Resources 171
    Paddlers Checklist 171
    Government Agencies 172
    Guides, Tours, and Rentals 174
    Fishing 176
Appendix B: Attractions 177
    Museums 177
    Other Attractions 178
    Lodging and Dining 180

Appendix C: Animals of the Everglades 182
    Birds 182
    Mammals 183
    Reptiles 184
    Amphibians 187
    Threatened and Endangered Species 187
Appendix D: Fishing in the Everglades 188
    Fishing Regulations: Freshwater and Saltwater 188
Suggested Books and Web Sites 191
About the Author 192

Overview

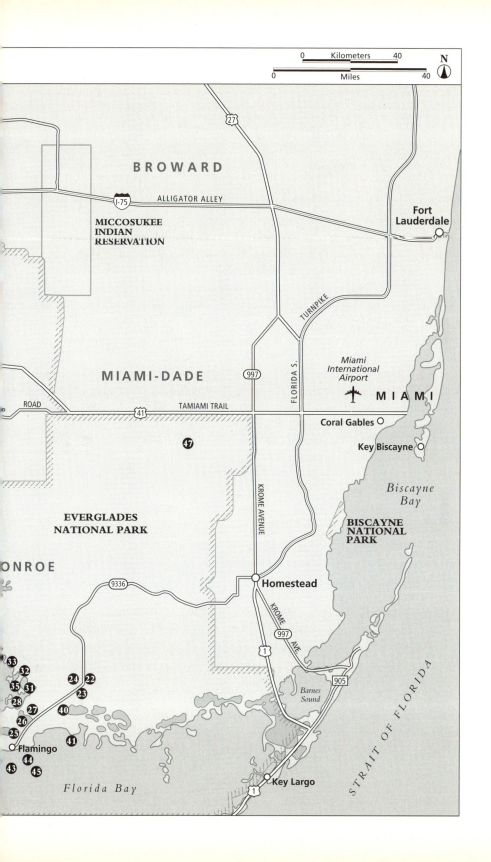

Acknowledgments

Writing a book is a team effort, similar to the efforts of a football team. You have the quarterback who calls the play, the author; the offensive team, in this case my guides; the defensive team, those who helped in fact checking and proofing; and the special teams, family for all their support and those individuals who went the extra yards in helping me put this together or make it through the goal posts. The coaches in this playoff game are my editor and publisher.

I would like to thank all these wonderful people for their patience, support, and assistance: Linda Frair, Bill Graf, Serena Rinker, Captain Charlie Wright, Captain Lauralee French, Edwin, Nicole and Owhnn (Everglades Hostel), Bob DeGross, Mike, Dr. Barry Rubenstein, Cherry Payne, Erik Egensteiner, Mark, Michael, Harold, Dr. Connie Mier, Tony Pernas, and Jack McNeel.

Also thanks to the staff at South Florida Water Management District, U.S. Fish and Wildlife, Florida Fish & Wildlife, The Nature Conservancy, Everglades National Park, the National Park Service, Big Cypress National Preserve, and the National Wildlife Refuge.

And to my husband, Todd, and my daughter, Ashley, *thank you both for your unending love and support!*

Introduction

Welcome to the Garden of Eden. The River of Grass. The Jewel of America. The Jungle. Welcome to the Everglades, where man meets Mother Earth.

The Everglades began forming 5,000 years ago when the sea level was rising due to increased rainfall.

Today the Everglades cover more than 14,000 square miles—from Lake Okeechobee in the north, Homestead on the East Coast, south to Florida Bay and the Gulf of Mexico, and west to FL 29 near Everglades City. Big Cypress National Preserve is on the northwest border of Everglades National Park.

Paddling is a great way to explore the Everglades—more than one-third of the park encompasses marine areas and estuaries under shallow water. Water birds, sea turtles, a variety of fish, and endangered manatees live in the park's waterways.

The best time to paddle in the Everglades or the Ten Thousand Islands is during the drier months, November through April. It is also cooler then, with less humidity and fewer pesky insects. However, the skies can still be sunny and the wind can suddenly pick up and be strong. Peak season is usually November through April. Hotels and campsites will be filled at that time, so plan ahead when scheduling your trips, including guided services.

It is possible to travel from the Everglades' headwaters down through lakes and the Kissimmee River, and into Lake Okeechobee. From here you can take the Miami Canal south toward Everglades National Park. Although you won't be able to paddle the entire route, it will still be a lifelong memorable journey as you traverse the Glades like the Indians first did, by hiking and canoeing through the swamp.

Please remember that collecting plants and animals in Everglades National Park is prohibited. This includes such things as orchids, air plants, seahorses, starfish, conch, tropical fish, coral, sponges, and driftwood (except for fuel). One quart of non-occupied sea shells may be collected per person.

Not all paddles are going to be round-trip. There are many routes, islands, and such worth paddling, and you can choose which trips you want to combine. Most, if not all, can be one-day events with a shuttle.

The Honorable Mentions section at the end of the book identifies the paddles that didn't make the cut, for whatever reason. In many cases it's not because they aren't great paddles, but because they're remote or environmentally sensitive to heavy traffic. Be sure to read through these. A jewel might be lurking among them.

I hope you enjoy many hours of paddling and viewing and that this guide is helpful to you. I hope you have as much fun paddling these routes as I have had compiling them. The friends I have made and the experiences I have embraced while researching this guide will stay with me for a lifetime. Come see the world through emerald-colored glasses with me.

Florida History

From Native Americans to farmers, southern Florida has been a political hot spot for centuries. Michael Grunwald's book *The Swamp* is a tearful journey of the destruction and possible resurrection of the Everglades. Grunwald chronicles how people first tried to drain and then reclaim the land and how the U.S. Army Corps of Engineers "tamed the beast with levees and canals, converting half the Everglades into sprawling suburbs and sugar plantations. The River of Grass stopped flowing and 90 percent of its wading birds vanished."

South Florida people migrated here about 11,000 years ago. They are believed to have been descendents of Paleo-Indians, who became known as the Tequesta on the southeast coast and the Calusa on the southwest coast. Both tribes built their villages at the mouths of rivers and on islands. They subsisted on shellfish, turtles, deer, small mammals, and wild plants. They hunted with nets and shells and canoes made from chiseled-out cypress logs. They used shells to create picks, drinking cups, chisels, fishhooks, and other tools. They used shark teeth to make knives and mud for making pottery.

The historical shell mounds, found on southern islands off the Florida coast and believed to have been burial and ceremonial sites, were originally just middens (refuse) of discarded shells.

During the early 1500s the Tequesta population numbered about 800; the Calusa numbered about 2,000. Spanish explorer Ponce de Leon arrived in 1513 while exploring for gold and slaves and stopped in a town called Manataca, present-day Cape Romano. The Calusa who were living here at the time had heard about Spanish cruelty from traders in the area. They fought long and hard, only to succumb to the Spaniards.

In 1565 Spanish Captain General Pedro Menendez de Aviles sailed to south Florida. His fleet was mired by storms, and the Spaniards holed up in a Tequesta village in Biscayne Bay. He returned in 1567 with soldiers who provoked the natives. A skirmish ensued in which an uncle of a Tequesta chief was killed. The infuriated Tequesta retaliated, forcing the soldiers to retreat.

The Spanish continued to establish missions and forts along the coasts to gain a foothold in the New World. Both the Tequesta and the Calusa suffered from the slave raids and European diseases, and the native population was reduced to a diminutive lot of survivors by 1800.

At the end of a long war, Florida became the property of the British in 1763 and Spanish missionaries and soldiers left the area. The Creek and the Muskogee Creek migrated to south Florida from the Carolinas, Georgia, and Alabama. This group became known as the Seminoles. By 1821 the Seminole population had grown to about 5,000. They not only made their living here but also aided slaves in their escape for freedom.

Forced to a small reservation north of Lake Okeechobee, the Seminoles struck back by raiding white settlements. When many Indians were forced by Congress in 1830 to relocate, creating the "Trail of Tears" to Oklahoma, the Seminoles declared war on the U.S. Army. Two wars, 1835–42 and 1855–59, resulted in severe losses on both sides. When the hostilities ended by truce in 1859, only 150 Seminoles were alive. Today this tribe, now known as the Miccosukee Tribe of Florida, still lives in Everglades National Park.

The Miccosukee were again pressured to leave their home by the white man's advancement and desire to develop the land. The Miccosukee persevered, retaining their native tongue language and family traditions and employing their both ancestral and modern skills to create a viable economy.

In 1821 Spain briefly took charge of Florida when the United Sates acquired the territory. A known haunt of pirates such as Black Caesar, the west coast was cleared by the U.S. Navy in the 1820s for salvaging ships.

Treasures were scattered among the reefs from shipwrecks caused by inclement weather and dangerous shipping lanes. Salvagers were entitled to a portion of the findings. Salvaging became a popular and lucrative business. Salvagers were entitled to a portion of the findings. More than forty shipwrecks are known to lie beneath the waters of Biscayne National Park. You can explore some of them through snorkeling or scuba diving or view their artifacts at the Maritime Museum.

Preserving the Glades

Indians, soldiers, and pirates were only the beginning of Florida's colorful and political past. Poachers and plume hunters found their way to south Florida, prior to the turn of the twentieth century, killing thousands of wading birds for their brilliant feathers and bringing great and snowy egrets close to extinction. In 1905 the National Audubon Society hired Guy Bradley to protect heron and egret rookeries. Bradley was killed safeguarding birds near Oyster Keys, but as a result of his death, people demanded protection for other colonies of birds. Paradise Key was granted protection by the creation of Royal Palm State Park in 1916.

Ernest F. Coe, a staunch supporter of protecting the Everglades, is responsible for Congress passing an Everglades park bill in 1934. Creation of the park was stalled by the Great Depression and World War II. Everglades National Park was finally dedicated by President Harry S. Truman in December 1947. Today Everglades National Park is a Wetland of International Importance, as well as a World Heritage Site and International Biosphere Reserve.

For decades loyal conservationists continued to strive for the safety of birds and protection of habitat in the park. Conservationists also helped keep developers at bay. In 1980 Congress authorized acquisition of Biscayne—complete with reefs, islands, and mangroves—to become Biscayne National Park.

Archaeology

Recent and ongoing surveys and archaeological sites have proved there is more than marginal or short-term habitat in south Florida. The plains region, south of Lake Okeechobee, was a transitional area used for canoe travel and small encampments by various tribes. Earthwork complexes have been found on the western edge of the Everglades. These sites show a strong affiliation with the Belle Glade area on the shores of Lake Okeechobee. Pottery remains found in the southwest section indicate influence from regions like Ten Thousand Islands and Florida Bay on the southernmost end. The settlement of south Florida has been chronologically categorized from 10,000 B.C. up to A.D. 1930.

Some scientists believe that from 10,000 to 8,000 B.C., the Paleo-Indians likely lived with mammoths, bison, and other megafauna in arid climate conditions. After the extinction of these animals, the Paleo-Indians adapted to the changing climate and established a subsistence culture of hunting deer and rabbit and gathering marine life.

During the next period, the post-glacial Archaic (8,000 to 750 B.C.), the sea level rose and diminished Florida's land, causing a climate change. Cypress swamps and hardwood forests of subtropical terrain began to develop. Resident peoples during this time would have relied on shellfishing, hunting, and gathering to survive. Enhancement of tools and pottery would have kept up with these new adaptations.

Next (750 B.C. to A.D. 1500) came the Glades periods I, II, and III, with different pottery types. A prosperous trade network is evidenced by exotic resources such as lithic tools and ornaments.

The Historic period (A.D. 1500 to 1750) included the arrival of the Europeans and the meeting of at least five tribes: the Tequesta in the southeast, the Calusa in the southwest, the Jeaga and Ais along the east coast of Florida north of the Tequesta, and the Mayaimi near Lake Okeechobee. It appears that the Calusa were dominant. It is also estimated that approximately 20,000 Indians resided in south Florida when the Spanish arrived. Unfortunately the population had been reduced to several hundred by 1763.

After the invasion of white settlers from the north, the Creek (Muskogee) people migrated southward for hunting and settling. During the Seminole Wars (1817–18, 1835–42, 1855–58), sovereign bands of Florida Indians established themselves in the Everglades to avoid removal.

South Florida coastal areas were still largely wilderness at the end of the nineteenth century. Florida was one of the last coastal regions east of the Mississippi to be settled. Chokoloskee, Cape Sable, and Flamingo were the only communities along the coast.

An Intricate Environment

Habitats and Ecosystems

Mangroves

It is in the mangroves where freshwater from the Everglades meets salt water from the tidal flats, creating a brackish estuary. It is believed that mangroves evolved from

Single and double (tandem) kayaks on the shore of Tiger Key with mangroves in the background.

freshwater flowering plants about seventy million years ago. Mangroves produce small white or yellow flowers, which are pollinated by large moths, bees, and wasps to form fruits. Live seedlings, called propagules, emerge from the fruits.

There are three types of mangrove trees in the Everglades: white, red, and black.

White mangroves thrive in the tidal waters, where freshwater from the Everglades mixes with salt water. It is able to adapt by two small glands on either side of the petiole or on the stem near the leaf. In extreme conditions the white mangrove will produce pneumatophores and prop roots like the black mangrove.

Red mangroves are the most tolerant of salt water. The red mangrove flowers most abundantly in summer. The flowers mature into pencil-shaped seedlings, or propagules, which sprout while still on the tree. Ripened seedlings drop off the tree and either land in the soft bottom below or are carried away by currents and tides. The buoyant seedlings can travel for months, bobbing along vertically in the water until embedding in a shallow area.

A "planted" seedling begins to develop prop roots and eventually grows into a tree. Prop roots help to stabilize the tree in water. Sand and decomposed plant and animals and sediment begin to collect around the roots. When sediments accumulate, other locations are created for more wandering seedlings.

Mangroves form the first line of defense for protecting the mainland from high tides and winds. They also provide shelter for wildlife and are a vital part of the food chain. Mangroves provide a nursery for shrimp, fish, crabs, and other marine life. Red mangrove prop roots provide shelter for marine organisms, including barnacles and coon oysters. Mangrove leaves provide a feeding ground for many species of wading birds. More than 220 different species of fish use the mangrove system, and more than 200 species of birds have roosted in the mangroves.

Black mangroves are easily distinguishable by their pneumatophores ("breathing" roots), which protrude from the ground. Black mangroves exude some salt but get rid of most of the salt in their tissues by secreting it through salt glands and fine hairs on the tops and bottom of the leave. The salt crystallizes on the leaves, and the wind blows it away. Many mangroves get rid of salt when they lose their leaves. Black mangroves are hermaphroditic, meaning both male and female flower types are found on the same tree.

Plant Communities

A unique freshwater ecosystem, today the Everglades covers almost 2,000 square miles (historically 4,000 square miles). Plant communities including saw grass prairies, open-water sloughs, and wet prairies span more than 70 percent of the remaining Everglades.

In the Everglades water slowly moves north to south through saw grass marshes before emptying into Florida Bay and the Gulf of Mexico. As you drive on I-75, known as Alligator Alley, you will have the opportunity to view a variety of habitats and some of the wildlife species these habitats support.

Saw Grass Prairies

Water levels vary in the saw grass prairies, with an average of 2 feet deep at the peak of wet season in October to below ground level at the end of the dry season in May.

HURRICANES

In 2005 the power of three—Hurricanes Katrina, Rita, and Wilma—wreaked havoc on Everglades National Park and the Gulf Coast states. Winds from Katrina, sustained at more than 125 miles per hour, hit the Flamingo area, damaging homes, visitor facilities, and the lodge. Later that fall, Hurricanes Rita and Wilma brought 8-foot storm surges along the same coastline.

Hurricanes have a considerable impact on the plants and animals in the park. However, they are a natural part of the ecosystem, having helped form the Everglades for thousands of years. Unfortunately, any debris in the water from hurricanes remains a hazard for boaters for a long time afterward.

The damage caused by these seasonal storms brings awareness to the need for focused preservation efforts. The Everglades are unique in the world. It is imperative that we preserve and restore the Everglades, for they preserve us.

Saw grass prairies are important to ground-nesting birds such as the endangered Cape Sable seaside sparrow and the American and least bitterns, which build elevated mound nests and use the saw grass for cover.

Open-water Sloughs and Wet Prairies

Open-water sloughs and wet prairies play an important role in the Everglades food web. During the rainy season, sloughs and wet prairies provide habitat for a wide variety of fish species as well as snails, crayfish, and other invertebrates. When water recedes in the marsh during the dry season, fish and invertebrates move to deepwater sloughs and ponds for refuge, providing wading birds and wood storks with a high concentration of prey.

Prairie/slough plant communities are threatened by the spread of nonnative plants like the melaleuca tree, originally introduced in the early 1900s to dry up the wetlands for development, and by invasive plants like cattails, which proliferate in areas with poor water quality. These plants easily out-compete native species and have little value for wildlife.

Willow Strands

Willow strands and large willow thickets, or "heads," are found throughout the area. Swamp willow is an important Everglades species capable of growing in shallow water and surviving long periods of flooding. Swamp willows are used by wading birds and snail kites for nesting. Colonial wading birds typically nest in large rookeries, where thousands of pairs of birds may occupy the same willow head. Conversely, snail kites generally nest in loose association with one another and prefer solitary willows or small strands in the middle of the marsh where visibility is restricted. For both types of birds, water under the nest tree helps protect their young from predators.

Tree Islands

Although tree islands make up only about 2 percent of the area, they are an integral part of the Everglades, providing critical habitat for snakes, deer, bobcat, raccoon, otter, marsh rabbit, and other small mammals. Tree islands also serve as nesting areas for alligators, turtles, and raptors such as red-tailed hawks. These teardrop-shaped islands generally run from north to south, following the historic flow of water. They can vary from less than one-quarter acre to several hundred acres, but are typically small in size.

Tree islands are susceptible to damage from fire during low-water periods. Historically, portions of the Everglades burned approximately once every three to five years as a result of lightning fires during the rainy season. The fires recycled limited nutrients back into the system and were beneficial to wildlife and plant communities. Under very dry conditions, however, soil-burning peat fires develop that are capable of burning entire tree islands down to below ground level. These dry conditions and related peat fires have increased in frequency as a result of development and increased water demands.

Pinelands

Pinelands are islands of higher, less-flooded ground with dense strands of broad-leafed trees and shrubs and surrounded by thousands of acres of open wet prairies. Pines in the Longboat Key area of south Florida were logged prior to the establishment of Everglades National Park in 1947. A network of 43 miles of paved and primitive roads created from the logging, fire roads, and old farm roads meander through the pinelands. Today these tiny trails, former roads of limestone bedrock, are used for hiking and biking.

From slash pine to saw palmetto, the pinelands are a diverse habitat containing more than 200 species of subtropical plants. This is also one of the last sanctuaries for the Florida panther.

As it does throughout the Everglades, fire plays an important role in the pinelands. Fires ignited by lightning burned through the pine forests every four to seven years. These fires kept the forest floor clean of fast-growing hardwoods that would otherwise grow and overtake the pines, destroying the diversity of the area. For the safety of visitors and local residents, prescribed burns have replaced the wildfires. All plants and animals in the pinelands and the Everglades are protected.

Flora and Fauna

The Everglades provide sanctuary for many species, from wading birds to unusual trees.

Birds depend on the climate's wet and dry cycles for breeding and feeding. The snowy egret, great egret, and roseate spoonbill live almost undisturbed in the Everglades along with other rare and unique avian species. The anhinga, often called the snakebird because it swims with its curved neck showing above water, also calls the Everglades home. The wood stork—endangered in Florida—is the only member of the stork family that currently breeds in North America. The American bald eagle is still threatened and the endangered snail kite also call the Everglades home.

More than 2,000 species of plants, both tropical and temperate, live side by side in southern Florida. Tropical trees such as palms, the "tourist tree" (gumbo-limbo), and mahogany grow in harmony alongside willows, pines, and oaks.

Some 572,000 acres of the Everglades are covered by saw grass and freshwater marsh, considered the prairie. A member of the sedge family, saw grass is the dominant plant species, creating a "river of grass" interspersed with sporadic hammocks—limestone outcrops supporting tropical plants and trees.

Ranging in size from a few feet to several acres, the hammocks are home to deer, raccoons, bobcats, barred owls, hawks, and marsh rabbits. Water moccasins, or cottonmouths (used interchangeably here), also live in this environment .

The strangler fig threatens trees by literally strangling their trunks. These parasites also steal the light, water, and nutrients of the host plant. Epiphytes, or air plants, on the other hand, may rest on another plant or tree but obtain water and nutrients from the air. The most popular epiphytes are wild orchids, which grow in hammocks with little light or cypress sloughs. The night-blooming epidendrum is pure white with spiky leaves and is one of the Everglades' most beautiful orchids.

A rare hammock resident is the liguus tree snail. These snails have a unique color variation, with patterns varying from orange and lavender to yellow and deep blue.

In the pinelands of Long Pine Key and the eastern Everglades, you can find slash pines, which are so hardy they grow in limestone bedrock. The pinelands are also home to saw palmetto, moonvine, and coontie (morning glory). This environment is inhabited by raccoons, pine warblers, opossums, cotton mice, and a species of reef gecko.

For more about Everglades fauna, see Appendix C: Animals of the Everglades.

The Moon and Tides

There are generally two high tides and two low tides each day, with about twelve and a half hours between the two high tides. When the sun and moon are aligned, exceptionally strong gravitational forces cause very high and very low tides, called spring tides. When the sun and moon are not aligned, the tides are not as dramatic; these are called neap tides.

Tides and Currents (Source: National Oceanic and Atmospheric Administration)

Tidal Station, Location	Latitude	Longitude	Mean Spring	Mean Range	Range Level
Chokoloskee	25° 48.8'	81° 21.8'	2.53	3.18	1.63
Everglades City, Barron River	25° 51.5'	81° 23.2'	2.26	2.84	1.47
Indian Key	25° 48'	81° 28'	3.4	4.3	2.3

PORT OF THE ISLANDS

Port of the Islands is located along US 41, also known as the Tamiami Trail, 20 miles east of Naples. This resort city of single-family homes, condos, a hotel, a restaurant, and a marina sits on the banks of the Faka Union Canal. This site, previously the Remuda Ranch, dates back to the 1950s and was only recently modernized in 2001. There is a concrete launch ramp near the marina; however, there is a fee to use the ramp.

The Faka Union Canal was constructed with other canals as part of the Everglades draining project in the 1950s for Gulf America Corporation's planned community. This community was to be 173 square miles, the world's largest subdivision. Auspiciously for Big Cypress Swamp, the company went bankrupt and the drainage was unproductive. For the past thirty years the government has been purchasing this undeveloped land for restoration.

This maze of canals has created environmental consequences for the Everglades. In Big Cypress Swamp the freshwater flows through the cypress and marshes toward the mangroves and bays of the Ten Thousand Islands in the Southern Golden Estates (Gulf America Corporation). These canals shunt freshwater from surrounding wetlands, mostly from west of Port of the Islands, into Faka Union Canal, which dumps into Faka Union Bay. This freshwater upsets the balance of the brackish water in the Ten Thousand Islands by dramatically lowering the salinity in bays to the west, starved of sheet flow, which is the natural flow of water in an area.

Present operation/restoration is removing roads and canals in the former development, now Picayune Strand State Forest. The flow of the Faka Union Canal will be reduced by up to 99 percent by redistributing sheet flow through natural waterways spread out over 20 miles of coastline. This will result in a healthier Ten Thousand Islands Estuary and, for paddlers, additional waterways.

The fresh, cool water from Faka Union Canal has attracted manatees, especially during winter and early spring. This area is relatively deep water, also great for manatees.

Paddling Equipment

Canoes and Kayaks

Most of the trips in this book are easy to navigate and great for novices. Canoes can be more difficult to paddle solo, especially when strong winds or tides come up on the waterways. It is always recommended that you go out with a partner.

Although canoes can hold more gear, kayaks are easier to paddle, and you can cover more water with less effort.

Kayaks come in a variety of styles and lengths. You will want to use the appropriate one for your trip. Longer, touring kayaks might be more difficult to navigate on smaller routes with tight mangrove tunnels.

Solo paddlers should use a canoe or kayak designed specifically for solo paddlers, and they should have experience paddling several miles in open water.

Sit-on-top kayaks are great for the Everglades because of the warmer weather and water. Kayaks with skirts on them help keep the sun, water, and uninvited guests from dropping in. They also have compartments for stowing gear.

Sit-inside kayaks are more comfortable than their sit-on-top counterpart. Some come equipped with rudders and skegs, useful tools for trimming and turning under difficult conditions. Like a weather vane, a kayak will align itself with the wind. Some kayaks tend to weathercock (point into the wind), and some tend to leecock (point with the wind). Putting a skeg down adds lateral resistance to the stern, giving the bow less resistance.

Kayaks come in light colors to help reflect the sun and keep it cooler inside. The brighter colors are easier for powerboaters to spot as they speed by. The plastic kayaks are inexpensive, easy to repair, and more durable against damage from oyster shells and the hot sun.

PFDs and Paddles

Personal floatation devices (PFDs) are required for everyone on the water, and there must be one per person on any boat. Even if you choose not to wear one, it should be readily available. Don't bury your PFD in a stowaway compartments or under too much gear.

Paddles are a personal preference. As you paddle the Everglades, you will encounter oyster bars, limestone, and mud. You will need a paddle that is lightweight, yet durable. You will be up a creek—literally—if you only have one paddle and it breaks or floats away.

Canoers will need a longer paddle for general use and a shorter one to help get through mangrove tunnels. Kayakers should bring two longer paddles and one short paddle for the mangrove tunnels. Most kayak paddles can be broken down and used feathered. This way you won't need another, shorter paddle.

A runaway kayak in the Ten Thousand Islands. If winds were present and you weren't there, your kayak would be long gone.

Charts, Compasses, and GPS

An accurate, current chart is essential for paddling the Everglades, as is a compass. A handheld Global Positioning System (GPS) device can be a great navigating tool on land or sea. GPS should not replace maps and charts, however, because you can lose satellite signals and batteries can fail.

Most mangroves, islands, and creeks tend to look identical, making it nearly impossible to navigate without the aid of a good chart and compass. You need to know the fundamentals of how to utilize both. Make sure the chart of the areas in which you will be paddling is both detailed and current. Due to hurricanes and other disasters, these charts can become outdated within a few years, especially for paddlers, which is also why it's a good reason to check with park rangers before embarking on a paddling trip.

Safety

The following tips can help ensure that your tales of the Everglades are of landing lunker fish and not of being rescued.

Carry all items required by the United States Coast Guard, including PFDs, on board your boat. Other suggested equipment: paddles, a bailer, bow and stern lines, waterproof bags for gear, a tide chart, a compass, water (one gallon/four liters per person per day), long-sleeved shirt and long pants for sun and insect protection, a wide-brimmed hat, shoes that can get wet, sunglasses, sunscreen, and insect repellent.

It is easy to become confused or lost while traveling through mangroves, so be sure to carry a nautical chart and compass.

Sudden storms can appear at any time. Check the weather and tides before leaving shore.

Leave a float plan with family or friends and check in with them to confirm you have returned.

Be prepared for mosquitoes during the summer months.

BOATERS RHYME

Remembering the following rhyme can help keep you from getting stuck or running aground:

Brown, brown, run aground! Avoid brown areas. This color indicates that a reef formation or sea grass bed is close to the surface.

White, white, you just might! Use caution. Sand bars and rubble areas may be much shallower than they appear.

Green, green, nice and clean! Green waters are generally safe for shallow-draft boats; larger, deeper draft vessels should exercise caution.

Blue, blue, cruise on through! Clear sailing in deepwater areas.

Camping and Launch Sites

Campsites

There are forty-seven campsites in the Everglades (see sidebar), including ground sites, beach sites, and chickees. (*Chickee* is a Calusa word meaning "a house with no walls.") Some campsites are currently closed to camping; check with the Park Service for status.

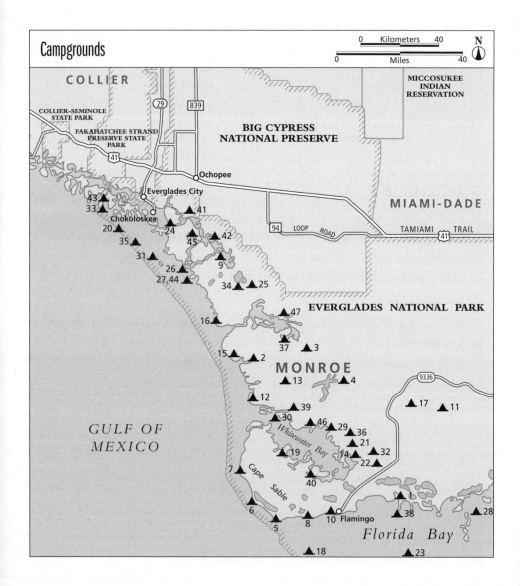

CAMPSITES IN THE EVERGLADES WATERWAYS

(Listed in alphabetical order)

1. Alligator Creek—ground
2. Broad River—ground
3. Camp Lonesome—ground
4. Canepatch—ground
5. Cape Sable, East—beach
6. Cape Sable, Middle—beach
7. Cape Sable, Northwest—beach
8. Clubhouse Beach—beach
9. Darwin's Place—ground (check for usage)
10. East Clubhouse Beach—beach
11. Ernest Coe—ground
12. Graveyard Creek—ground
13. Harney River Chickee
14. Hells Bay Chickee
15. Highland Beach—beach
16. Hog Key—beach
17. Ingraham—ground
18. Johnson Key Double Chickee
19. Joe River Chickee
20. Jewel Key—beach
21. Lane Bay Chickee
22. Lard Can—ground
23. Little Rabbit Key—ground
24. Lopez River—ground
25. Lostman's Five—ground
26. Mormon Key—beach
27. New Turkey Key—beach
28. North Nest Key—ground
29. North River Chickee
30. Oyster Bay Chickee
31. Pavilion Key—beach
32. Pearl Bay Chickee
33. Picnic Key—beach
34. Plate Creek Chickee
35. Rabbit Key—beach
36. Roberts River Chickee
37. Rodgers River Chickee
38. Shark Point Double Chickee
39. Shark River Chickee
40. South Joe River Chickee
41. Sunday Bay Chickee
42. Sweetwater Chickee
43. Tiger Key—beach
44. Turkey Key—beach
45. Watson Place—ground
46. Watson River Chickee
47. Willy Willy—ground

Everglades National Park sustained major damage from Hurricane Wilma. Kingston Key Chickee was destroyed. Broad River was also heavily damaged, and may still be closed at publication time. Carl Ross Key has suffered severe erosion and is currently closed to overnight camping. Check the following Web sites for additional information:

Camping and overnight permitting: www.nps.gov/archive/ever/visit/campsite.htm
Map of campsites: www.nps.gov/archive/ever/visit/camps2.htm
Backcountry campsites: www.nps.gov/archive/ever/visit/camps3.htm

Wilderness Permits

Wilderness permits are required for all overnight camping, except in auto campgrounds or when sleeping aboard boats. There is a fee for processing the permit. Permits may be obtained in person up to twenty-four hours before the day your trip begins. Please display your permit on your tent. Upon completion of your trip, turn your permit in at a ranger station or visitor center. Write any comments or complaints on the back of the permit, and report any violations to a park ranger.

Insect conditions are so severe during summer months that wilderness use is minimal and permit writing desks may not be staffed. Permits are still required, however. Follow the self-registration instructions at the Flamingo or Gulf Coast Visitor Center or the Key Largo Ranger Station (usually May to November).

Winter wilderness users originating from the Florida Keys will be able to obtain permits by calling (239) 695-2945 no more than twenty-four hours prior to the start of their trip for the following locations only: North Nest Key, Little Rabbit Key, Carl Ross Key, and the Cape Sable Beaches.

Permit fee required plus additional fees for each person.

Winter Hours

Gulf Coast Visitor Center (Everglades City)
8:00 a.m. to 4:30 p.m. daily
(239) 695-3311

Flamingo Visitor Center (including all Florida Bay sites)
8:30 a.m. to 5:00 p.m. daily
(239) 695-2945

Main Entrance Station (12 miles southwest of Homestead)
9:00 a.m. to 5:00 p.m. daily

Wilderness permits are written from the Main Entrance Station only for two land sites in the Long Pine Key area: Ernest Coe and Ingraham Highway.

Boat Ramps

Boat ramps are located at Flamingo, West Lake and Little Blackwater Sound on Key Largo, and City Seafood in Everglades City. There is also a ramp next to Outdoor Resorts on Chokoloskee Island and a canoe ramp at the Gulf Coast Visitor Center. Use of most ramps requires a boat launch fee.

Map Legend

Transportation

- 75 — Freeway/Interstate Highway
- 41 — U.S. Highway
- 29 — State Highway
- Other Road

Trails

- ------ Paddling Trail
- → Direction of Travel

Water Features

- Body of Water
- Major River
- Minor River or Creek
- Channel
- Canal
- Waterfalls
- Marsh
- Mangrove

Symbols

- Boat Launch
- Bridge
- Building/Point of Interest
- Campground
- Canoe Launch
- Marina
- 44 Numbered Trail Marker
- Picnic Area
- Start/End
- Ranger Station
- Visitor Center/Information

Land Management

- National Forest, State Parks & Wilderness Areas

Collier-Seminole State Park

1 Blackwater River Trail

The Blackwater River is spacious enough for canoes, kayaks, and small powerboats to paddle, fish, or cruise. As you paddle down the mangrove-lined channel and leave civilization behind, a sense of peace will flow though you. Listen as a variety of birds serenade you; smell the fresh air and absorb the calm habitat. Keep a sharp eye out for camouflaged birds, fish, and mammals. History can be found via remnants left after years of neglect and abuse. Canoe rentals are available from the ranger station at the park entrance.

County: Collier
Start/End: Collier-Seminole State Park launch ramp, 20200 E. Tamiami Trail, Naples, Florida, 34114
Distance: 13.0 miles round-trip; 6.5 miles to Palm Bay into Ten Thousand Islands; 13.0 miles round-trip on left, marked waterway
Approximate float time: Most of the day
Difficulty: Easy to moderate paddling; great for novices and families
Nearest town: Naples
Season: Fall, winter, and early spring
Fees: State park entrance fee
Hazards: Wind, current, motorized boats
Highlights: Birds, including woodpeckers and swallow-tailed kites; oyster bars with redfish, snook, and big sea trout; flying fish (mullet); dragonflies; Grocery Place and Old Grove
Getting there: The entrance to Collier-Seminole State Park is off US 41 (Tamiami Trail). Collier-Seminole State Park is 17 miles south of Naples. Heading south from Tampa on I-75, take exit 101 (FL 951 and FL 84) and turn right. Turn left on US 41 and then Collier-Seminole State Park will be 8 miles on the right just past CR 92.

Coming west from Ft. Lauderdale, take exit 80 (FL 29), go south to 41, and turn right. Follow US 41 for about 15 miles and Collier-Seminole State Park will be on your left. The ramp is inside the park. Follow signs to boat launch, about 0.5 mile in. Register at the ranger station: (239) 394-3397.

The Paddle

Collier-Seminole State Park is a versatile 7,271-acre park located approximately 17 miles south of Naples.

As you launch from the boat ramp (basin), the water is calm and you are flanked by mangroves on both sides. The channel is at least 20 to 25 feet wide, shared by powerboats and canoes. The mature mangroves, both red and black, provide a nursing ground for fish and other creatures.

This long tunnel of red and black mangroves meanders for 6.5 miles, with winding curves along the way. Short tunnels, or honey-holes, branch off, offering shaded areas for viewing or fishing. Some areas are shallow enough that you can get out of your canoe or kayak and stretch your legs, but there is no real area for picnicking.

Follow the markers. Number 56 marks the end of the canal and the beginning of the natural waterway. Continuing south, the channel narrows about 500 feet from

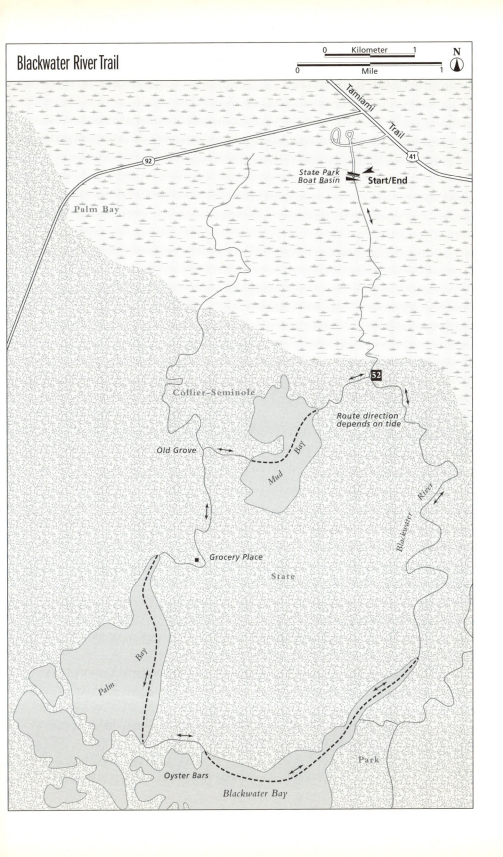

marker 54. Follow the waterway west to Marker 52, where canoers are directed to the left. The river alternately narrows and then widens as the mangroves form a canopy over you then open up to beautiful skies.

Moderate traffic will allow you to stop and enjoy the serenading of birds (along with the rat-a-tat-tat of woodpeckers). By late April/early May, most migratory species have started back north.

After Marker 49, the river takes a sharp left turn, heading east. The river widens again around Marker 47, which indicates the confluence of the Blackwater River with a creek heading west to Mud Bay. Watch for shallow water, especially near shore, where sand and mud will ground you quickly.

Option (1): During shallow water take the left fork and head down Blackwater River. Paddle south following the turns all the way down to Blackwater Bay. This route can be beautiful with mangroves and serenading prairie warblers. You will encounter a few sharp turns along this route. However, you may also encounter fallen trees, overgrown mangrove tunnels, and spider webs. Once you reach Palm Bay, depending on the water depth, you can return the way you came, heading north this time on Blackwater River, or, if the water is high enough, you can paddle around in a clockwise directionand make the loop up and into Mud Bay.

When you reach Palm Bay, you will want to paddle west following the mainland (on your right). Here you may encounter dolphins and oyster bars. This is also a great place for fishing. When the land makes a sharp right, follow this up and the lake will narrow into a river and then smaller as you head up to Grocery Place. It's best to stay along the east shore as you paddle north. When Palm Bay narrows to a creek, you are about four miles from the launch/put-in/take-out. As you paddle up, look for remnants of an old house or store on your left (west shore); this will be Grocery Place. This is a good place to get out and stretch if needed. Also, this serves as a primitive campsite. From here paddle southeast around the point and then head back north up the creek. On your left will be marked Old Grove; here you may see spotted sandpipers, white ibis, and egrets as you head into Mud Bay.

Option (2): Where the river comes to a fork, stay to the left; channel markers will guide you. When the tide is high, you can take the right fork at the confluence, heading into Mud Bay. You'll find Mud Bay appropriately named if you try to paddle it any time other than high tide.

The channel narrows for a while and then opens up again to about 50 feet across. Continue through Mud Bay, staying to the west side and being sure to avoid the mangrove island in the center. Mud Bay is often shallow; skirt along the perimeter as necessary to avoid the mud and look for water channels.

Mud Bay is approximately 2.5 miles from the boat ramp/marina. Scout around for wading birds such as egrets and ibis that hunt the mudflats. The outlet of the bay is at Old Grove (3.0 miles from the marina).

Continue heading southwest through a wide channel. Enjoy more solitude as you stay to your left through the mangroves interspersed with sable palm trees. Follow

The beginning of the canal is flanked with mangroves; red, white, and black.

the bends in the creek until you come to Grocery Place on your right. This is a good place to stop and stretch, but be careful of the drop-off and roots. This area occasionally serves as a primitive campsite.

From here you will paddle around the point, heading south and then turning northwest and circling Grocery Point. Remnants of an old building can be seen on your right.

Resume paddling in a corkscrew manner. Where a smaller creek comes in on your right, stay to the left on the main stream, moving toward yet another bay. The creek widens as you enter Palm Bay. You may want to stay near the left shore, heading south toward Blackwater Bay. Like Mud Bay, Palm Bay is shallow and muddy.

Stay to your left as you go through Palm Bay so that you don't miss the channel into Blackwater Bay. Winds will make your trek difficult—they will be coming from the bay, making the water choppy. As you go through Palm Bay, keep the mainland on your left so that you don't get disoriented in the labyrinth of mangrove islands on your right.

The bay narrows as you head east. Take a sharp turn and follow the mainland. You may encounter wildlife while paddling this stretch, heading north-northeast. You will come to several places where you can split into open bay or other waterways, but don't. Stay heading north. The oyster bars in this area are great for fishing and you can reel in redfish, snook, and sea bass. Indigenous birds and other wildlife will be abundant here, cohabitating in the mangroves.

You are now in the open Blackwater Bay. Don't be surprised if you happen on frequent boat traffic here. Continue paddling east until you reach markers again. You will then be heading north into Blackwater River, around Marker 11. Keep a watchful eye for oyster bars, manatees, and river otters, as well as bald eagles and roseate spoonbills. You may also encounter swallow-tailed kites from February through August and prairie warblers.

You have paddled about 7.0 miles now. Follow Blackwater River north and paddle through mangrove tunnels and fallen trees. Stay on the main river channel as the river makes a few sharp turns west and southwest.

Crab traps are common along the bay and in the river. Smaller branches and creeks join the river. The mangroves on either side of the river offer a little shade and comfort. Follow the channel back into the boat basin.

This loop is about 13 miles. You will want to keep an eye on the tide before heading out. If you're at low tide, paddle south on the Blackwater River and then head through Palm Bay and north around the loop to Mud Bay and back to the boat launch.

Port of the Islands

2 Faka Union River Route

Beautiful flora and fauna as well as history will embrace you as you paddle down the canal. Keep a sharp eye out for bald eagles, ospreys, purple martins, manatees, and alligators, which are part of the local color. Enjoy the junglelike mangroves, buttonwood trees, orchids, and crustaceans along the route. Bring your charts, bird or flower checklists, a journal, binoculars, a camera, and possibly a picnic lunch to complete your excursion.

County: Collier
Start/End: Port of the Islands Marina
Distance: 11.0 miles round-trip
Approximate float time: Most of the day
Difficulty: Mild to moderate paddling
Season: Fall and winter
Fees: Small fee for boat ramp
Highlights: Mangrove tunnel, flowers, manatees, and other wildlife
Hazards: Winds and tides
Getting there: Port of the Islands is located between Naples and Everglades City, off US 41. From Naples head east on US 41 (Tamiami Trail). Drive 13.5 miles from the intersection with CR 951. Turn right at the main entrance before the bridge. The marina will be on your left.

From Everglades City drive about 13 miles, first north on FL 29, 3 miles up to the intersection at US 41, then turn left, heading west towards Naples for about 10 miles. Turn left at the main entrance on the west side of Faka Union Canal.

The Paddle

Launch from the marina and head down the canal. You will need to go more than 2.0 miles before you even reach the river. However, there is plenty of wildlife to see as you head out. You may see bald eagles, ospreys, purple martins, manatees, alligators, and a variety of fish.

As you paddle down the canal, you will see smaller creeks taking off to your left. If it is late in winter, these little streams may be dried up. One creek has a beached boat wreck. You will reach the mouth of the Faka Union River at 2.5 miles from the marina. There is a large buttonwood tree at the mouth of the river; past this point the canal turns and heads southwest.

You enter a mangrove tunnel as you paddle down the river. The waterway meanders east, northwest, and then southeast. Continue paddling along the red mangroves, which seem lifelike here. You may see some small crustaceans.

Eventually the mangroves open up and the river becomes shallow, with a sand bottom. Along the way you will see buttonwood trees, orchids, and epiphytes. Be careful if you take any of the side creeks off the main channel. They lead to smaller ponds; however, you might get lost.

The river makes a turn to the west about 3.5 miles from the launch. You then need to select a route, either left or right. The right leads to a dead end, so take the left

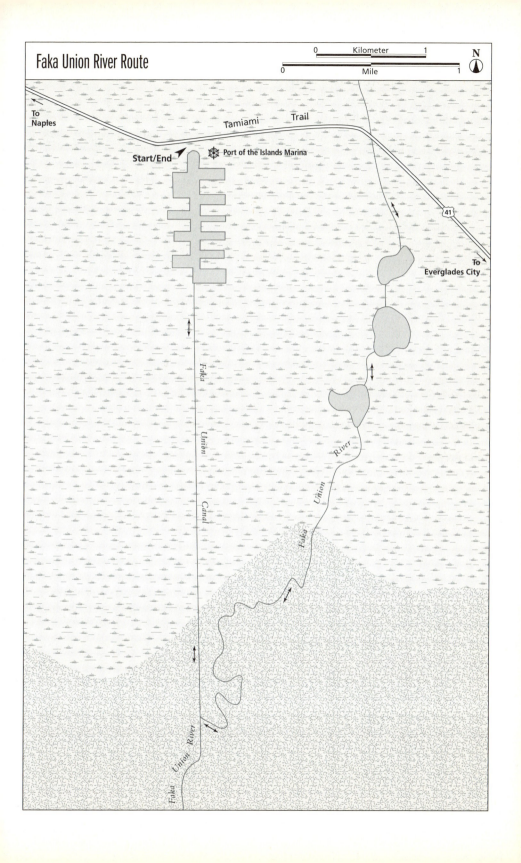

Paddlers enjoy a leisurely float through mangroves and marsh.

fork. After paddling 0.5 mile you will come to a chain of lakes. This is the northern part of the river. These lakes may be shallow, especially at low tide, but they contain mullet. Paddle north to meet up with another lake. At one point you can stand on the grassy shoreline and look out at the marsh and mangroves across to US 41. You may see wildlife such as bald eagles, ducks, and gators along here.

Begin paddling back when you have gone 5.5 miles from your launch site. Retrace your route, heading southwest through the lakes and back to the river. The mangroves offer nice shade on your return, and you'll be paddling with the current. When you reach the mouth of Faka Union River again, 3.0 miles downriver, it's only 2.5 miles north up the canal back to the marina.

The Western Everglades

3 East River Canoe Route (Fakahatchee Strand State Preserve)

This route is a standout. If you enjoy diversity of landscape, then you will enjoy the views of the prairie as well as paddling or pulling your way under and through the mangrove tunnels. The maze of tunnels can be alluring for some, intimidating for others. You will also encounter an abundance of wildlife, from birds to crustaceans. Depending on when you visit, you may encounter egrets, white ibis, herons, and red-shouldered hawks. Time your paddle for when you have plenty of light and time to find your way around, in case you get disoriented. You will also want to keep an eye out for crocodiles.

County: Collier
Start/End: US 41 (Tamiami Trail); gravel canoe ramp off the side of the road, approximately 5.2 miles from the intersection of US 41 and FL 29
Distance: 5.0 to 6.0 miles round-trip to Fakahatchee Bay; 12.0 miles round-trip to Everglades City
Approximate float time: 4 to 8 hours, depending on how far you want to go
Difficulty: Easy to moderate paddling; difficult navigation
Nearest town: Everglades City
Season: Fall and winter

Fees: None
Highlights: Mangrove tunnels, prairies, birds, and other wildlife
Hazards: Oyster bars, tides, narrow channels, spider (nonpoisonous) webs, crocodiles, and crab pots during winter months
Getting there: From Everglades City drive north, then west approximately 5 miles from the intersection of US 41 (Tamiami Trail) and FL 29. Or follow US 41 about 18 miles east from its intersection with CR 951. Look for a gravel drive to the edge of a pond. Parking is limited; you may need to park off the side of the road.

The Paddle

Launch your canoe or kayak in the small pond off the gravel put-in and head southeast. The put-in is marked with red tape on prop roots and flagging tape. You soon come to your first mangrove tunnel. Pass through the tunnel into an opening and then turn to the left, continuing through another small tunnel.

After winding through the mangroves, you will come out into a long pond. Turn right and follow the pond south, with saw grass prairies on your right and possibly other vegetation, such as ferns, beyond the mangroves. About 0.5 mile down, you will reach a pond. Stay to your left and enter another tunnel; when you come out into and the open again, bear right. This tunnel may be hard to find. Look for red markings or where the water is flowing. This tunnel is longer than the others along the route.

After coming out of this long tunnel into a small pond, continue paddling until you reach a larger pond. This larger body of water, Lake #1 on the park map, is about 1.5 miles from the launch site. This lake is the most northern of the chain.

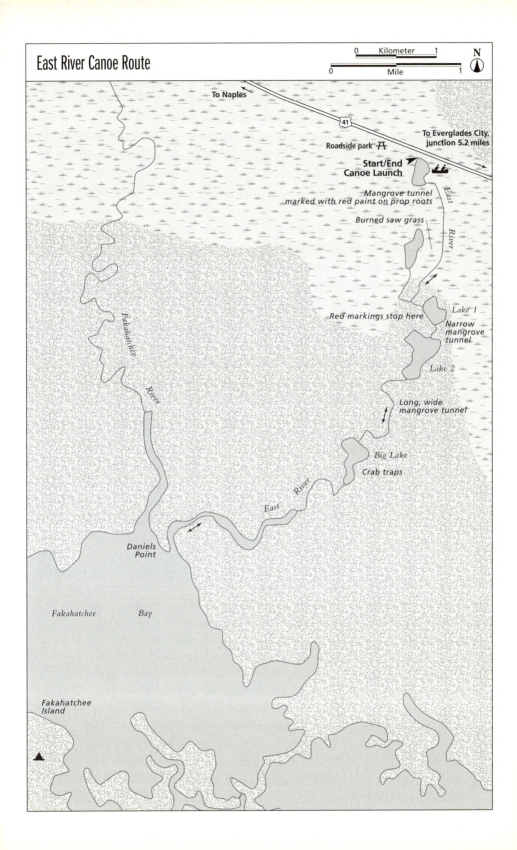

A variety of ecosystems can be found in the Everglades. This is a sawgrass prairie.

Head south-southeast across the pond, which narrows and enter another tunnel. The canopy of this tunnel is higher and there is a plethora of epiphytes and Spanish moss.

The tunnel comes to a T at a large buttonwood tree. Take the left fork and continue down the tunnel, keeping an eye out for downed trees (snags). This mangrove tunnel contains drop roots and meanders and twists around for about 0.5 mile. At the end of the tunnel, you will enter another lake, Lake #2 on the map. Cross the lake, heading about 240 degrees, and look for another tunnel at the end.

This tunnel, the longest on the route, heads southwest for about 1.0 mile to Big Lake. The water depth may be deeper here than in the previous tunnels, and the bottom may be muddy. Here you will notice the air roots (pneumatophores) from the black mangroves. Looking like snorkels or periscopes, they help aerate the trees' root systems. You may see white ibis, red-shouldered hawks, and mullet in this tunnel. The tunnel widens toward the end and you emerge into Big Lake (Lake #3).

Paddle across this lake, heading south-southwest. Big Lake may be shallow and will contain crab traps. Be careful not to paddle this section at low tide. It will be muddy and difficult to maneuver. (Option: Big Lake is your turnaround point if you prefer the shorter route with the mangrove tunnels and lakes.)

At the southwestern corner of the lake, you will see a lagoon on your right. This lagoon leads to several mangrove tunnels that can take you to Fakahatchee River to your west. You may encounter crocodiles in this lake and possibly mullet. Continue paddling south, where the lake narrows to a wide channel of the East River. This is the last section before Fakahatchee Bay. If it is low tide, just look for the flow from the main river and continue downriver. Stay to the west side and enjoy the scenery. Traditionally this river has mud bars along the route. You may see spotted sandpipers and, occasionally, greater yellowlegs.

Try to stay in the main river and avoid the mud bars. You may also want to keep an eye out for crocodiles, which will race into the water to avoid you. Don't worry—they usually don't charge people unless provoked. However, you still want to give them a wide berth. The deeper water is on your right, or the river's west edge. The river narrows as it flows west. If you need to stretch your legs, the mud should be firm enough at low tide at the bend where the river turns south.

At about 3.75 miles, you will see a smaller channel shooting off to the left. This will take you to a shallow lake. Paddle on through and stay on the main river. As you continue paddling downriver about another 1.0 mile, you should see some oyster bars along the banks—a sign that you are approaching the mouth of the East River, Fakahatchee Bay, and Daniels Point.

The river is flowing south-southwest now. Before entering the mouth, the river shifts slightly and heads south-southeast. With the water flow, you should be able to paddle between the oyster bars and make it to Fakahatchee Bay, or you can continue down the main channel. You are now about 5.0 miles from the put-in.

Daniels Point is northwest when you reach the bay. Take a sharp right and stay along the shoreline. You only have to paddle about 0.25 mile to reach the point, on your right. Daniels Point, an old shell mound, is great for stopping and resting. You should be able to pull up here for a while to stretch. Other than some pesky no-see-ums, there isn't much here. From here you can paddle across the bay to Fakahatchee Island.

It is believed that settlers inhabited Fakahatchee Island as far back as 1870. The island was used for farming and the locals fished the area. A school was built on the island in 1912, attended by thirteen students. The Daniels family lived on the island until the 1960s.

To reach the island, paddle south-southwest, a compass reading of about 210 degrees, from Daniels Point. It is less than 1.0 mile to the island from the point. Because of its shape, you should be able to see the island from the shell mound. You should be able to pull right up to the island. There are gumbo-limbo trees and a cistern in this general area—as well as mosquitoes and no-see-ums. Also keep an eye out for barbed wire cactus.

You can paddle around to the east side of the island, past some pilings, to another landing. From here you can walk on a little trail to a cemetery. The trail is lined with tropical hardwoods and exotic plants. You may find some pigeons here as well. Both the plants and remains here have historical significance. Please don't remove anything or deface it in any way.

Paddling around Fakahatchee Island adds 2.0 miles on your route. From the first landing near the cistern, head out at a compass bearing of 40 degrees to return to the mouth of the East River. The landscape may appear different, even though you are just reversing your route. The change of tide alters the appearance of the landmarks and landscape somewhat. You may see tarpon as well as mullet as they launch themselves out of the water—some may even land in your canoe or kayak.

Once you get back to Big Lake, a heading of 30 degrees will help you find the mangrove tunnel you came out of earlier. Paddle or pull your way through the chandelier-like mangroves. As you exit the tunnel into Lake #2, follow a heading of 60 degrees across the lake to the next tunnel. This is the tunnel with draping red mangrove drop roots and the T junction with the buttonwood. At this point, turn right and head north. (Going straight at the T will take you to a tangle of roots that will block your path). Paddle through this tunnel and emerge into Lake #1. Head north across the lake and take the second opening, ahead and to your right. At an opening in the tunnel, stay to the left.

At the end of the tunnel, paddle north, 20 degrees. This will take you to the connector tunnel, which in turn takes you to the long canal. Continue north for another 0.5 mile. After passing a bay on your right, look to your left for the flagging tape directing you to the tunnel that will take you back to your launch area and the borrow pond.

After exiting the connector tunnel, paddle 315 degrees northwest. There will be a little island ahead; keep it on your right. This mangrove shoreline offers some good fishing for snook and small tarpon.

4 Turner River (Big Cypress National Preserve and Everglades National Park)

This is another of my favorite paddles—a kaleidoscope of natural beauty in a serene, tranquil setting. Cypress, maple, and palm trees line this route in addition to flowering plants, river otters, egrets, ibis, and great and blue herons. I enjoyed riding along this route in a canoe with a group led by a park ranger. Guided tours are especially eye opening and appealing with a small group.

These routes are great for kayaks, as the mangrove tunnels can be tight, muddy, and layered with snags. Watch for turtles and other wildlife along the way. Take pleasure in the labyrinth of mangroves that are a thriving habitat for a variety of birds, fish, and other creatures that call the Everglades home. This route will take you out to Chokoloskee Island or to see Calusa shell mounds for an amazing day trip.

County: Collier (Big Cypress National Preserve)
Start/End: H. P. Williams Roadside Park; near bridge on US 41 (Tamiami Trail)
Distance: 7.5 miles one-way, up to 16+ miles round-trip
Approximate float time: 6+ hours
Difficulty: Easy to moderate paddling
Nearest town: Everglades City
Season: Fall and winter
Fees: None
Highlights: Mangrove tunnels, diverse habitat, orchids; occasional river otters, egrets, ibis, great and blue herons; possible anhinga and osprey sightings
Hazards: Low branches, shallow water, snags; occasional alligators; airboat channels in the saw grass prairie. Some tunnels may be cluttered with debris; spider webs are common. Paddlers may encounter winds and waves on Chokoloskee Bay.
Additional information: During certain times of the year, the Upper Turner River does not have enough water to paddle. Check with Big Cypress National Preserve for current conditions. Ranger-led programs may be available through Big Cypress during the winter months.
Getting there: From Everglades City drive north on FL 29 to US 41. Turn right onto US 41 and head east for about 6 miles to a parking area on the northwest side of the bridge.

The Paddle

Launch in shallow water from a short ramp near the highway. Flora and fauna welcome you. This is a great river for beginners, as the water depth goes from 18 inches up to 12 feet as you come to Chokoloskee Bay. There is very low current at the beginning of the route and through much of the waterway. As you paddle under the bridge, go slow to enjoy the anhingas, herons, egrets, and other birds, along with alligators and flowering trees. Cypress, maples, and sable palms line the banks.

Paddle through abundant cypress trees and freshwater vegetation, including water lilies, for about 0.5 mile until you come to the first mangrove tunnel. As you pass through this fascinating labyrinth of mostly red mangrove trees, put your paddle inside your kayak or canoe. Use your arms and hands to pull yourself through this vital mangrove web. If you are quiet, you may observe river otters tottering through the forest.

This 0.2-mile tunnel opens to a small pond. Look to the right for a second tunnel, a little longer than the first. During winter, when it may be drier, watch for shallow water and roots underneath your canoe or kayak. These tunnels are a kaleidoscope of natural beauty with blue skies, reddish-brown water, and green vegetation.

The Turner River route heads south on your right. The old Turner River Canal is visible to the left. This canal was built in an attempt to drain the swamp. It has since been plugged to restore natural water flow.

After the tunnel the waterway widens. The trail continues straight as saw grass prairies flank the boat. This is a great place for a picnic. Look around for alligators and osprey nests.

Paddle through the saw grass and come to a small pond with hydrilla, cattails, and wading birds. The trail appears to go straight along the mangroves, but it doesn't. The canoe trail veers off to the right and enters a mangrove tunnel. This tunnel is 0.4 mile

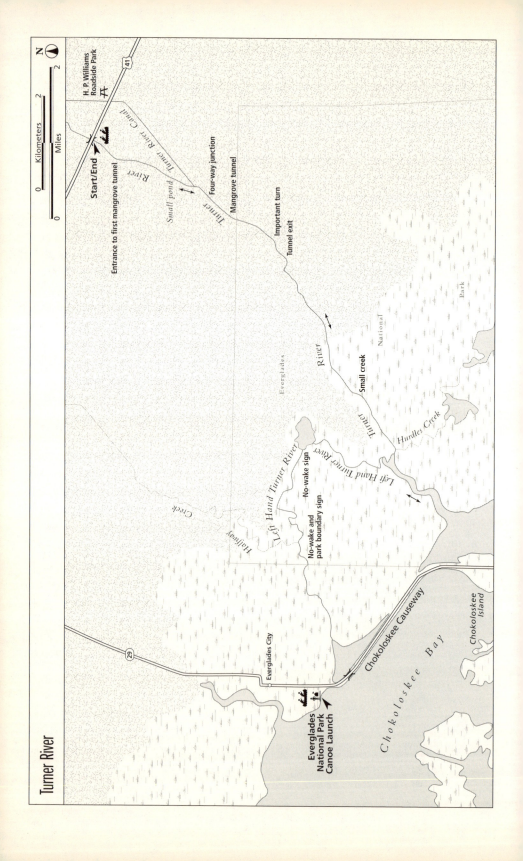

long with arched roots, a lower ceiling, and many air plants. At this point you will have gone approximately 1.75 miles. You should come across a marker designating the border between Big Cypress National Preserve and Everglades National Park.

As you paddle out of the tunnel, the river widens and you pass through a series of lakes. Turner River can be very quiet and you can get out and stretch your legs along the open, or pond, areas. Continue south to a small creek, great for birding and looking along the shorelines for turtles and tall cabbage palms. The water is about 4 feet deep, with a sand bottom.

Beware of powerboats as you continue on, reaching Hurdles Creek (on your left, when heading south) at about 5.75 miles from the put-in. Chokoloskee Island is approximately 2.5 miles downriver. Left Hand Turner River (actually on your right as you head south), approximately 6.0 miles from the launch site, will take you to Halfway Creek.

Enjoy more mangrove tunnels along the way. Halfway Creek trailhead is located along Seagrape Drive. Calusa shell mounds can be seen near here. Also look for Florida's popular "sea cows," or manatees.

You can turn around in one of the various ponds or lakes along the river or travel down to Chokoloskee Bay (8 miles from the launch site) and continue on into Ten Thousand Islands. Reverse direction from the bay and retrace your route for a 15.0-mile round-trip (16.0 to 17.0 miles round-trip when connecting the Halfway Creek and Turner River Canoe Trails).

The launch for Halfway Creek Canoe Trail is 4 miles west of the Turner River launch site, or 2.25 miles east of the intersection of FL 29 and US 41.

5 Halfway Creek

NOTE: Parts of this route have not been cleared since Hurricane Wilma in 2005. You cannot paddle this entire route. You can go as far as Marker 7 when coming from Seagrape Drive. From there you can take the loop to Barron Lake, described below.

For this route you may want to leave your vehicle at the takeout and have someone drop you off at the put-in. Halfway Creek is a brilliant blueway that offers a variety of birds, dolphins, mangrove tunnels, and shell mounds. You can paddle from the Seagrape Drive put-in to Chokoloskee Bay. This will take you to the Turner River or to Plantation Island, where you can see remnants of an old homestead.

County: Collier (Big Cypress National Preserve)
Start: Everglades National Park (ENP) canoe ramp or Seagrape Drive, off US 41 (Tamiami Trail). Your put-in and takeout will depend on the tide. For the described route, the put-in is at Seagrape Drive and the takeout is at the national park canoe ramp.
End: Everglades National Park, Gulf Coast Ranger Station canoe ramp
Distance: 11.0 miles one-way

Approximate float time: All day
Difficulty: Easy to moderate paddling
Nearest town: Everglades City
Season: Fall and winter
Fees: None
Highlights: Birds, dolphins, mangrove tunnels, Calusa shell mounds
Hazards: Possible strong currents and difficult navigation
Getting there: From the intersection of FL 29 and US 41 (Tamiami Trail), go east on US 41 about 2.5 miles. Turn right just before the Big Cypress National Preserve headquarters. To get to the ENP ramp from the intersection of FL 29 and US 41, head south on FL 29 for 3 miles to Everglades City, then follow the signs through town and around the traffic circle, following signs for the Everglades National Park. Turn right into ENP; the canoe launch is behind the park service building.

The Paddle

This attractive route takes paddlers from the Seagrape launch southwest to Chokoloskee Bay or from the Everglades National Park launch and north up toward Seagrape Drive, depending on the tide. Paddlers will need to leave a vehicle at one end for the return trip or arrange for someone to shuttle them back.

Enjoy a leisurely paddle from the Seagrape Canal launch site. Along the banks you will see mangroves, cattails, and Florida's limestone bedrock—*La Florida*'s foundation. This easy paddle will allow you the opportunity to see freshwater vegetation, as well as a few former airboat trails (airboats no longer travel on this waterway). You may also see wading birds feeding in the shallow water.

Seagrape canal leads to a lake and into Halfway Creek. Markers designate the canoe trail, and pine trees offer shade. Follow the markers south-southwest along Halfway Creek. A small creek leads off the right to Barron River. Stay on the main waterway, which alternately narrows and widens as it meanders south to the bay.

Continue paddling, following the markers. Around Marker 6 you will come to mangrove tunnels. You may need to put your paddle in your canoe or kayak and use your hands to pull yourself through, along the air plants. At this point you are almost 3.0 miles from the boat launch.

You may see another marker (L1), near Marker 7. This right turn will take you to the New Halfway Creek/Barron River Loop. Go past this marker and continue east along the creek and then south again. Paddle at an even speed, watching for low-hanging branches above as well as those lying in the water. At Marker 9 you will be at the intersection of Halfway Creek and Left Hand Turner River. Left Hand Turner River goes east to Turner Lake. Continue on Halfway Creek as it continues to narrow

◄ *Seagrape Drive park ramp. Park rangers offer guided tours and canoe rentals.*

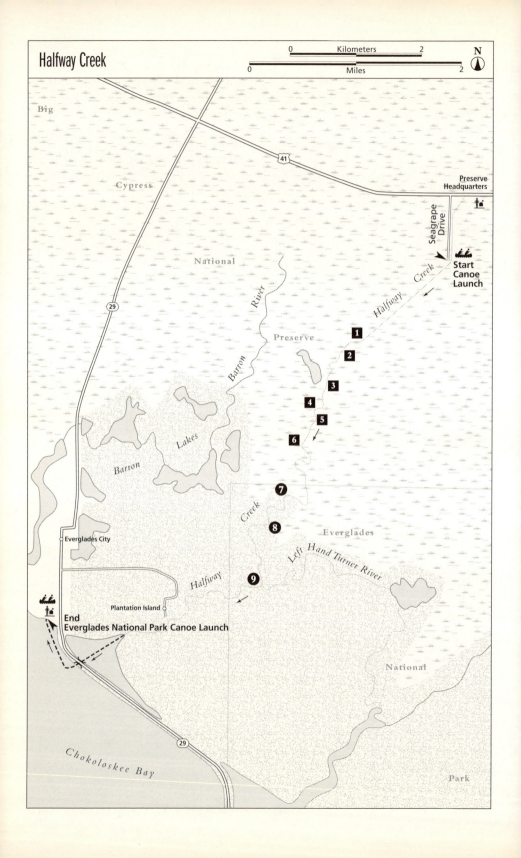

into a canopied creek and then widens. The tunnel ends near Plantation Island, on your left.

In this area, among the mangroves are remnants of old homesteads and cisterns. You may see some Brazilian pepper (an exotic species that has been mostly removed from Sandfly Island), Australian pine, and buttonwood trees.

Continue paddling toward the bay. As you head southwest you will paddle under a bridge. Keep an eye on the tide, which can be swift in this area. After passing under the bridge, head northwest toward the ranger station on your right. Your takeout for this direction is the Everglades National Park canoe launch.

6 Halfway Creek to Barron Lakes Loop

NOTE: Halfway Creek is partially blocked (from Marker 7 to Marker 9) due to storms. You can paddle to Marker 7 and return or do a loop.

This is a picturesque blueway with some difficulty. The canal is surrounded by saw grass prairies, red mangroves, and limestone. The marked route meanders between ponds and mangroves. Highlights of this trip include manatees and fishing. Ferns and buttonwood trees offer visual respite along your sojourn's peaceful path.

County: Collier (Big Cypress National Preserve)
Start/End: Seagrape Drive canoe ramp
Distance: Approximately 8.5 miles
Approximate float time: 6 hours
Difficulty: Moderate to difficult paddling
Nearest town: Everglades City
Season: Fall and winter
Fees: Fishing license if you are going to fish
Highlights: Mangrove tunnels and shrubbery, occasional manatee; marked trail (green markers on the way out to the Gulf, red on the return trip)
Hazards: Strong current
Getting there: Halfway Creek is in the southwest corner of Big Cypress National Preserve. The launch is on US 41 (Tamiami Trail), about 2.5 miles east of the junction of US 41 and FL 29. Turn south onto the gravel road and follow the road to the canoe ramp.

The Paddle

Launch from the Seagrape ramp, an easy, leisurely paddle. Along the banks you will see mangroves, cattails, and Florida's limestone bedrock—*La Florida's* foundation. This easy paddle will allow you the opportunity to see freshwater vegetation, as well as a few former airboat trails. You may also see wading birds feeding in the shallow water.

Seagrape canal leads to a lake and into Halfway Creek. Markers designate the canoe trail and pine trees offer shade. Follow the markers south-southwest along Halfway Creek Canoe Trail. This is an old canal.

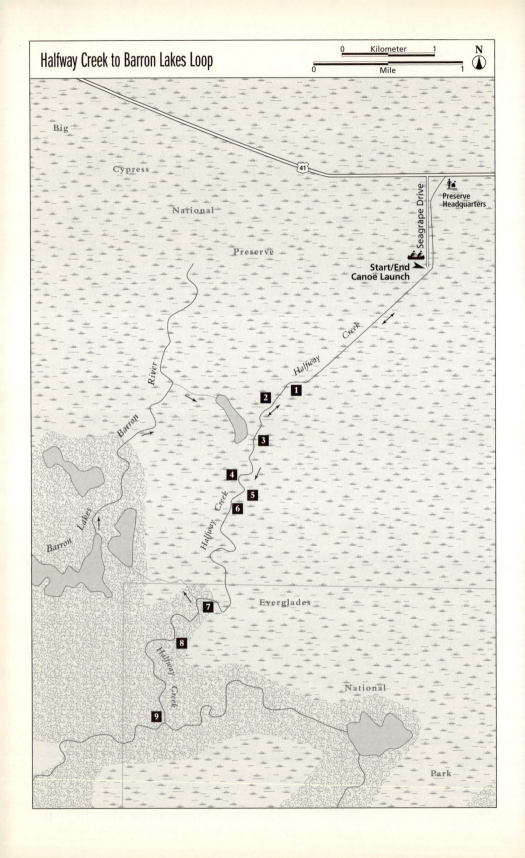

Paddle approximately 3 miles, following the markers for Halfway Creek. The water is deep here and lined with limestone boulders. Saw grass prairies surround the canal and red mangrove trees dot the edges. You may see alligators and crab traps.

It's best to head south when the tide is going out so that the return trip will be easier to maneuver. The canal alternately widens and narrows during the first few miles. Small feeder creeks branch off to the right or left but don't go anywhere. Mangrove tunnels encase you. The trail begins to intermingle between ponds and small river ways, and cabbage palms and buttonwoods appear sporadically.

Continue paddling to Marker 7. Veer off to the right here, away from the marker, into another tunnel. Look for Marker L1. You will follow Markers L1 through L15 on this journey.

You are now heading west, with a few turns northwest; the creek widens. Leave the creek and head west through a mangrove tunnel, which then winds around and takes you into Barron Lake. Continue following the creek north and enter a pond. Continue west, meandering into yet another pond. The creek is lined with mangroves and ferns, offering a beautiful view as well as some solitude. Follow the minor twists and turns along the waterway.

Paddle northwest and head into a bay. You are now on the Barron River lakes. Continue paddling along the shore to the next lake, heading north-northeast. A turn to the left will take you to the chain of lakes. You don't want to go this way. Instead continue heading straight in the creek, which bends with some canopying but soon opens up again.

A narrow passage is ahead; take this north. Enter another tunnel and then paddle into the open. Come to an area where you need to choose between following a wider creek or making a sharp left. Take the wider creek north into a pond, and then paddle northeast to stay in the river.

The creek bends to the right and left. You have paddled about 6.0 miles by now. As you enter another pond, go to the right, south and then east. The route is lined with mangroves, almost canopied. Relish spending time in nature among the buttonwoods and air plants along the banks as you head back southeast. Branches enclose the creek for a brief time and then you're in the open again. Cabbage palms along the banks occasionally lean out over the water. Serpent ferns grow along the base of the palms.

Keep paddling a few hundred more feet and enter a bay encircled by palms. This pond should be relatively shallow, although picturesque with mangroves and saw grass. From here you want to paddle east across the bay, giving a little room around the island on the southeast corner. A small island with cabbage palms and air plants lies along the left bank. Continue padding into a short creek, where you will intersect Halfway Creek Marker 3. Turn left and paddle up Halfway Creek. Bear right at Marker 2. As you come to Marker 1, you will see Seagrape Canal, then a pond. Just beyond the pond is Halfway Creek. Paddle up the Seagrape Canal for about 1.0 mile to the canoe ramp.

EVERGLADES CITY

Everglades City has friendly townspeople, great food, comfortable lodging, an accurate historical museum, and a unique 1800s rod and gun club. There are several guide and adventure companies in town—one at a bed-and-breakfast, where guests can rent equipment and even find a spa to soothe sore muscles.

A two-story wooden observation tower near the visitor center is a great place to get a bird's-eye view of the area, but they don't seem to keep regular hours. Commercial crab fishermen inhabit the area, although their numbers are dwindling due to the impact of development and pesticide runoff.

THE BARRON RIVER

Originally known as Potato Creek because of the growth of potatoes along the riverbank, the river was narrower, shallower, and winding. Later the waterway was called Allen's River and then the Barron River, named for Barron Collier after his purchase of Everglades City. The west fork runs almost parallel to FL 29, from north of Everglades City to Carnestown on US 41.

7 Barron River, West Fork

This paddle is both challenging and fun. You will encounter powerboats; a variety of birds, fish, and mammals; and a maze of mangroves to peruse. Paddle northeast through tunnels, zigzag through lakes, and finally enter an area where airboats used to roam free. Take a compass, your chart, and look for trees or other markers to help you remember your return path. Be prepared for great photo opportunities on this trip for wildlife, wildflowers, and wilderness.

County: Collier
Start/End: City Seafood ramp, 702 Begonia St., Everglades City
Distance: Approximately 7.0 to 8.0 miles round-trip
Approximate float time: 4 to 5 hours
Difficulty: Mild paddling
Nearest town: Everglades City
Season: Fall and winter
Fees: Launch fee at boat ramp
Highlights: Manatees, mangroves; birds, including purple martins, blue-winged teal, swallow-tailed kites, and bald eagles
Hazards: Powerboats
Additional information: The National Park Service visitor center is located approximately 1 mile south from the start/end location. Rentals and ranger-led trips may be available during the winter season.
Getting there: Everglades City is approximately 2 miles south from the intersection of FL 29 and US 41 (Tamiami Trail). There used

to be a Barron River Marina, which also had a fee to launch. The ramp is still there; however at the time of writing this guide, it wasn't open to the public. Everglades City Seafood is just off of FL 29 as you head south on FL 29; turn right onto Begonia Street and the restaurant and launch will be on your right.

The Paddle

You will be paddling north-northeast on this route.

Brown pelicans are the sentinels of the signal (marker) board, and a pair of sea cows will occasionally play near the dock. If you leave early, purple martins and other birds may serenade you.

Turn right and paddle under the bridge, keeping to the left bank to avoid airboat tours. When you reach the Park Service marker, turn left, heading east-northeast to head north on the river. Follow the river as you paddle north and then east for almost 2.0 miles. The river appears to dead-end.

Turn right and follow the river as you head east and then turn again, heading northwest as the river widens. Dense stands of red mangroves line the banks. The west

The Barron River is busy with powerboats and anglers.

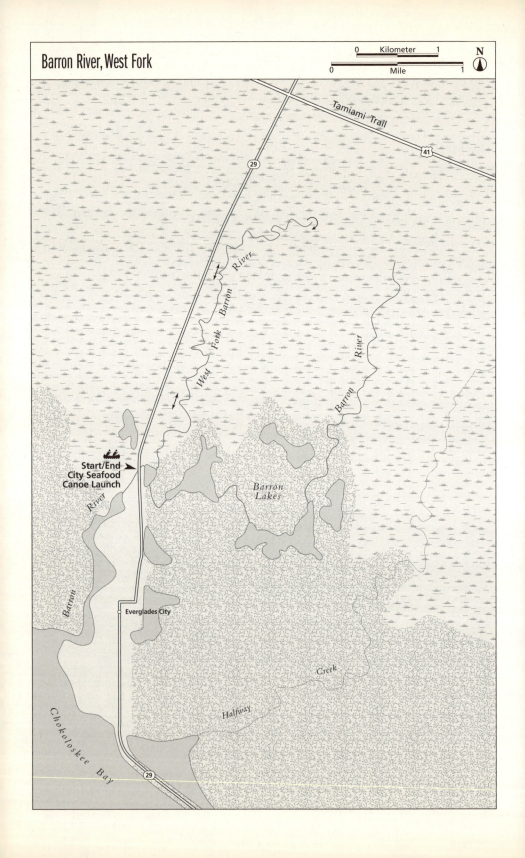

branch of the river winds around east and northwest, running almost parallel to FL 29, less than 0.25 mile away. Continue paddling along the main branch of the river as smaller creeks appear to the right or left.

About 2.25 miles from the marina, come to a mangrove tunnel to your right. The river takes you east and then southeast and then widens. When the river forks, take the left channel, heading northeast. (The right fork dead-ends.) The river splits again and may become shallow and muddy. Look where the water flow is stronger, and follow this current from east to north. Along the way you may encounter blue-winged teal or swallow-tailed kites feeding in this area.

Follow a zigzag waterway east and north and eventually reach Carnestown. This area has prairies, cabbage palms, mangroves, wax myrtles, and swamp bays—traditional Everglades. Enjoy the wildflowers and solitude. You may see old PVC pipes that airboat tours once used for markers. Turn around here and head back the way you paddled up, reversing your heading to south-southwest. This area may be a little confusing, so be sure and use a compass and chart on the way up to help identify your way back.

Chokoloskee Island and Everglades City

In 1910 Everglades City had a population of 144, many of whom were farmers.

Chokoloskee, near Everglades City, was first settled in the 1870s. The home of Calusa Indians for centuries in pre-Columbian times, it became the trade center for homesteaders throughout the Ten Thousand Islands region.

One hundred and forty-four people in twenty-nine different households made up the 1910 census for the Everglades township and Chokoloskee Island. Many were farmers or farm laborers and most were probably engaged in the labor-intensive growing of sugarcane. There was also one carpenter, a mail carrier, a washwoman, a sailor, and a schoolteacher. Two men made their living as merchants—Charles "Ted" Smallwood and George Storter.

The Everglades-Chokoloskee community was just recovering from a hurricane in 1909 when it was devastated by another, the worst on record, the following year. Only the highest ground of the old Calusa shell mound remained above water. Low-lying farm fields were salted by flood tides and most cisterns were polluted—a major tragedy in an area with few springs or wells. Many inhabitants of the outlying islands were forced to abandon their homesteads. The most infamous incident of the times, the killing of Mister Watson—the vigilante murder of a local man suspected of several murders—occurred a few days after the hurricane.

The only way to reach Flamingo or Chokoloskee was by boat. Supplies came in from Key West, Fort Myers, or Tampa; cane syrup, fish, and produce were traded in return. Some Chokoloskee produce is reported to have reached New York City.

Everglades City was flourishing in the 1920s when Barron Collier made it his headquarters for building the Tamiami Trail across south Florida. It served as the county seat of Collier County until 1960, when prosperity waned and county offices were moved to Naples. Neighboring Chokoloskee did not have a road until a causeway was built from the mainland in 1956.

8 Barron River, East Fork

This is a pleasant, easy paddle with some nesting birds along the way. You will take different forks along the river, paddling in a leisurely loop. Enjoy the short jaunt as you view the wildlife.

County: Collier
Start/End: Barron River launch site, off FL 29
Distance: About 4.0 miles round-trip
Approximate float time: 2 to 3 hours
Difficulty: Easy to moderate paddling
Nearest town: Everglades City
Season: Fall and winter

Fees: Launch fee at boat ramp
Highlights: Lakes, wildlife, birds
Hazards: Boat traffic, wind, tides
Getting there: Follow FL 29 south 3 miles (before Begonia Road on the right) from US 41 (Tamiami Trail) to Everglades City; the start/end will be on your left. The gravel put-in is off FL 29.

The Paddle

Launch from the gravel just off FL 29. Follow the river past the national park marker and turn right to enter the east fork. Continue on this route, heading south and east. Head south approximately 0.5 mile and then meander your canoe or kayak northeast. Continue paddling until you come to a fork, the first of several forks in the river. Take the east channel.

Come to a small lake 1.3 miles from the marina. The river leads to the north, and you soon enter the first of several lakes. This is a nice route for exploring the habitat as you paddle along. You may see osprey and other nesting birds.

Return the same way you came in.

SUNSET PADDLES

These paddles are offered as guided trips in the Everglades City area by the Ivey House (North American Canoe Tours) and Everglades Eco Tours. These popular excursions are offered daily during the winter months, allowing paddlers to enjoy the beauty of the mangroves and saw grass. You put in prior to sunset and travel quietly until reaching the open prairie. You will then take a break, have a snack, and watch the sun slowly recede in all its glory. You will see various birds flying overhead and nesting for the evening, including wood storks, ibis, egrets, and herons.

After the sun sets, paddlers put on headlamps; glow sticks also are available. You can shine your light along the river's edge and see red or yellow eyes glowing back at you. A full moon provides a luminescent glow and an aid to navigating on the way back.

For more information or to schedule a tour, call the Ivey House (239-695-3299) or Everglades Eco Tours (239-695-4666).

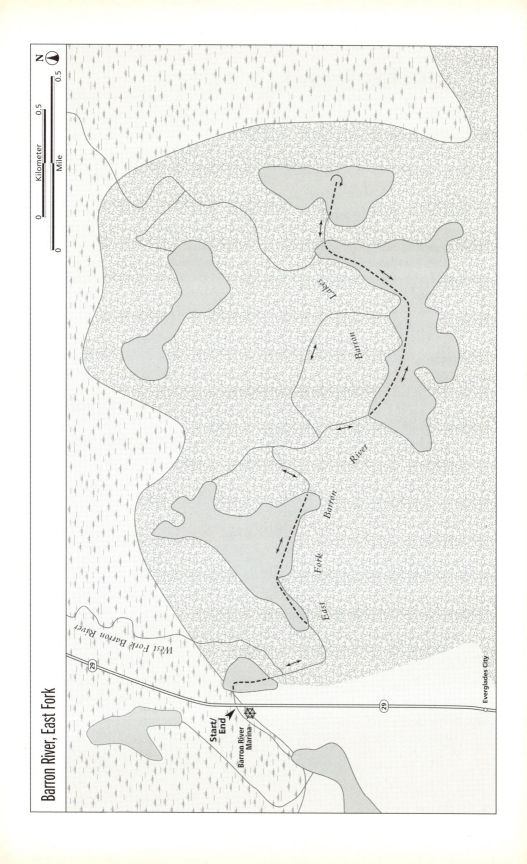

9 Barron River to Seagrape Drive Ramp

This paddle provides a slightly more challenging workout with wind, tides, and boat traffic along the route. As you paddle through lakes and enjoy a scenic island tour, you will encounter mangrove tunnels, cabbage palms, and a variety of plants.

County: Collier
Start: Boat ramp behind City Seafood
End: Marina on Seagrape Drive
Distance: Approximately 6.0 miles one-way
Approximate float time: 3 to 4 hours
Difficulty: Moderate to difficult paddling; difficult navigation
Nearest town: Everglades City
Season: Fall and winter months

Fees: Launch fee to use ramp at City Seafood
Highlights: Marsh, mangroves, Halfway Creek
Hazards: Wind, strong tides, boat traffic
Getting there: From the intersection of FL 29 and US 41 (Tamiami Trail), head south on FL 29 for 3 miles into Everglades City. The boat ramp is behind City Seafood, 702 Begonia St., Everglades City.

The Paddle

From the boat ramp, follow the Barron River east. Turn right (you should see a marker designating you are in the park), and go under the bridge. Stay to one side to avoid airboat tours and stay to the right of the marker. The river is wide for about 1.5 miles. Follow the river into a few lakes, where you can enjoy some bird watching. Ospreys nest along the river here.

Paddle north in the lake, which narrows into a creek. Do not paddle east into the next lake; instead stay in the creek to go to Seagrape Drive. (**NOTE:** Follow this creek with an incoming tide.) Here you will intersect the Halfway Creek and the Barron Lakes route. Turn right into this lake and enjoy. Continue paddling to your right to stay on course, heading northeast, and after a few hundred feet a tunnel will lead away to the right, but be aware that this is a dead end. Instead head north and northwest another ¼ mile to a small pond (you have paddled about 3 miles from the launch) and then northwest into a mangrove tunnel. Throughout the tunnel look for buttonwoods and other trees, air plants (epiphytes), and candy coral.

The creek narrows as the mangroves enclose it for a while and then opens up again.

You have traveled about 3.5 miles at this point and may see a marker in the water. Stay to the left and continue paddling as the creek narrows. When you come to another small pond, paddle southeast. You will need to make a turn to the northeast at a point where you will see several cabbage palms.

Continue paddling until you reach another fork, with a choice of heading north or east Take the east channel and head southeast toward the bay of Halfway Creek. Come to another pond after a few hundred more feet. Paddle southeast through a few

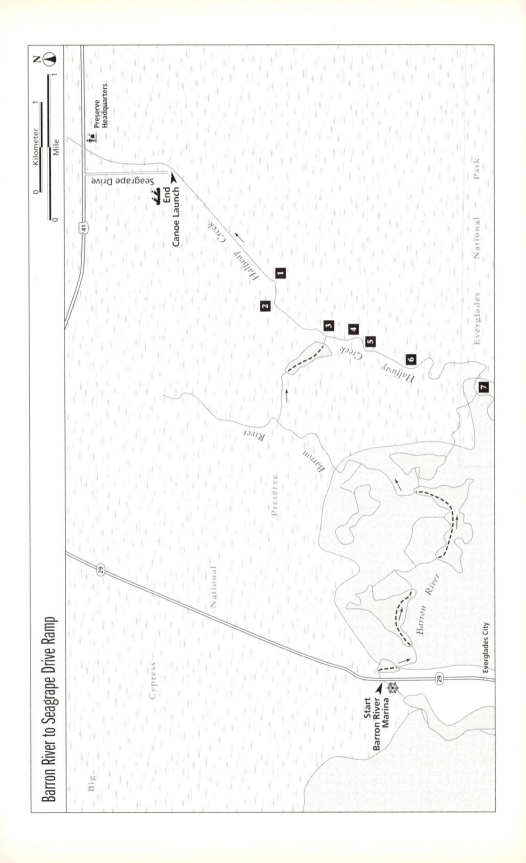

Chokoloskee Island is popular for both anglers and pelicans.

more ponds, which will be encircled by more cabbage palms and mangroves. About 4.0 miles from the put-in, you will see a cabbage palm with a woodpecker hole and ferns growing around it. Paddle east from this point.

You will reach the first of Halfway Creek's bays about 4.5 miles from the put-in. Paddle southeast from here. The bays are fairly good size and surrounded by mangroves. Paddle east through the lake and around a little island with palms. Follow a small creek, which will take you to Halfway Creek at Marker 3. From here turn left and paddle up Halfway Creek. Enjoy the scenic beauty of palms, buttonwoods, and orchids. Ignore any smaller channels that veer off the main river; these will dead-end. You will see a few markers and should see Seagrape Canal up ahead. This bay is at the headwaters of Halfway Creek. Follow the canal for about 1.0 mile to the canoe launch off Seagrape Drive.

Ten Thousand Islands

10 Sandfly Island

This wonderful, historical route includes Calusa Indian relics and a 1.0-mile nature trail with boardwalk on Sandfly Island. As you depart from the boat ramp, you may encounter some boat traffic, but you'll soon reach a tiny island where you can explore for crustaceans and see red, black, and white mangroves. You may even see dolphins as you paddle.

County: Collier
Start/End: Everglades National Park Ranger Station, Gulf Coast
Distance: 5.25 miles round-trip
Approximate float time: 3 hours
Difficulty: Easy to moderate paddling
Nearest town: Everglades City
Season: Best in fall and winter
Fees: Launch fee, paid at ranger station
Highlights: Dolphin sightings, cistern, gumbo-limbo trees (aka: tourist trees), boardwalk, Calusa Indian relics, and swallow-tailed kites, osprey, and other birds
Hazards: Tides, wind, motorized boats
Getting there: From the junction of US 41 (Tamiami Trail) and FL 29, follow FL 29 for 3 miles south to Everglades City. Continue through town, following the signs to Everglades National Park and Chokoloskee. The canoe launch is behind the park headquarters building.
Additional information: Canoe rentals and guided tours are available at park headquarters.

The Paddle

Depart from the sand/dirt ramp behind the park headquarters building. As you paddle out into the channel, you may see dolphins frolicking near the markers as you head west.

Approximately 0.25 mile out is a small sand island where dozens of ocean creatures are born, nurtured, and play their part in the food chain. This miniscule island is inhabited by one each of the three types of mangrove—red, white, and black—entwined with one another. The black mangrove has pneumatophores (black roots that protrude upward through the sand, providing air the tree needs to survive).

Spend a few minutes shell surfing for a few of the indigenous crustaceans, including coon oysters, stone crabs, and crown conchs. Unfortunately, because the channel is very busy with motorized boat traffic, this island may no longer be conducive to exploring.

Reboard your canoe or kayak and keep heading west-southwest, staying to the right. Continue paddling past Markers 2 and 1, following Sandfly Pass. On your right will be Sandfly Island, best known for its middens—and of course the sand flies (also known as no-see-ums). There is a small area to pull up on the sand, or you can pull in next to the wooden dock and port-a-potty. The water near the dock is usually about 8 feet deep. For safety reasons, canoes and kayaks should tie up to a mangrove rather than to the wooden dock.

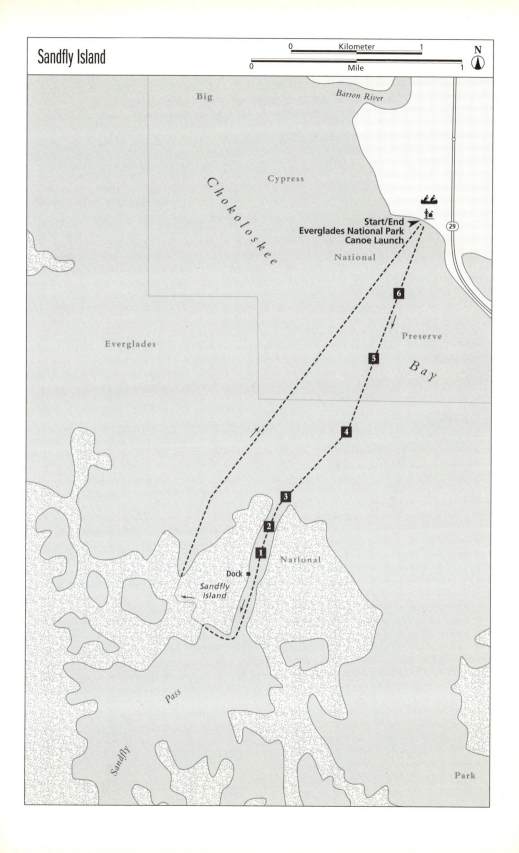

This 1.0-plus-mile-long island once was home to the Calusa Indians. The Calusa were nomads who knew how to utilize natural resources. For example, they built a horseshoe-shaped mound, or weir, on the western side of the island. The tide brought in fish and oysters, enabling the Calusa to catch their dinner with little effort. The ancient shell mounds provide multiple layers of treasures, full of history and fascinating discoveries.

A 1.0-mile nature trail begins from the dock. The loop trail is alive with fauna and flora such as a wildlife pageant of tomato plants, wild coffee, and pigeon plums. Hidden in the hardwood hammock, you will find a cistern used in years past. As you meander along the trail, touch the tourist tree (gumbo-limbo). The tree is tall, straight, and cold to the touch. It appears red and has very thin (almost transparent) layers of bark peeling off. Underneath the transparent bark, the tree is green. Other notable trees along the trail are royal poincianas, mangroves, and white stoppers, a tree that gives off a slight odor.

The Park Service has graciously put in a boardwalk that allows visitors to partake in the natural beauty while viewing several species of birds, including swallow-tailed kites, oystercatchers with their bright orange bills, ospreys, skimmers, and pelicans. It's not unusual to see more than thirty different bird species on one outing.

You can certainly return the way you came; this is especially helpful if the tide is going back in. Or your can continue your trek around Sandfly Island, going south around the tip, then west and north back up to the launch site. From the canoe tie-up on the island, head south along Sandfly Island around the southern tip; this is a scenic paddle. Turn to your right towards the inlet and follow the land (island).

Here you may see snowy egret, great egrets, little blue herons, and possibly swallow-tailed kites. Continue paddling through this pass it will get narrower and the current may increase. Follow this northeast and then it hooks back around northwest. Follow along with the mangroves until you come to a cut (opening) in the mangroves, at which point you will veer to the right to get to Sandfly Pass, which is cut in the open waterway. Head north-east across the bay. Paddle north into and through Chokoloskee Bay (about 1 mile across) to the canoe launch.

11 Gopher Creek

NOTE: Reprinted and modified, with permission, from Dr. Connie Mier; http://cmierphotoandfitness.net/everglades.html.

This route, popular for ecotours, is great for birding, fishing, and photography. This fascinating paddle will bring you to a historical site, Watson Place, via the Chatham River. The actual put-in for this paddle is an hour away from land but well worth it. Or, to save time, you can get shuttled by powerboat via the bay. You may want to pack in gear to camp for a night and visit Darwin's Place. (**NOTE:** Darwin's Place may be closed due to vandalism; check with the park ranger before heading out.)

County: Collier (Ten Thousand Islands)
Start/End: City Seafood or Park Service boat ramp. The start of the paddle is a one-hour (one-way) ride by powerboat (shuttle) from either boat ramp, carrying your kayak, equipment, etc., into mangrove backcountry.
Distance: Approximately 9.0 miles round-trip from Watson Place down to Darwin's Place. Approximately 12+ miles if you continue through Cannon Bay, Gopher Creek to the Gulf, and then back through Chatham's River to Watson Place.
Approximate float time: Watson Place to Darwin's Place-9.0 miles: 3 to 4 hours. Around the Gopher Creek Rate-12+ miles: 4 to 6 hours depending on the tide. If leaving from ENP boat ramp, add another 15+ miles each way.
Difficulty: Mild to moderate paddling
Nearest town: Everglades City
Season: Fall and winter

Fees: Launch fees for City Seafood and Park Service boat ramps; shuttle fee to and from the mangrove backcountry
Highlights: Great for birding, photography, fishing; Calusa Indian relics
Hazards: Wind, current, boat traffic, mosquitoes
Campsites: Darwin's Place, Watson Place
Getting there: If launching from City Seafood ramp (702 Begonia St. Everglades), from Naples take Tamiami Trail (US 41) east to the intersection with FL 29. Turn right and head south to Everglades City. City Seafood is down about 3 miles on your right; turn right onto Begonia from FL 29. To save time, prearrange for a powerboat ride to Darwin's Place from the City Seafood or national park ramp. The ENP is approximately 1 mile south from City Seafood. Follow the signs though town, around the traffic circle and down, and turn right into the ENP Gulf Coast Station. The ramp is behind the headquarters building.

The Paddle

This spectacular paddle takes you from the Barron River southwest toward the Gulf, near Chokoloskee Island and up into the Lopez River, through Crooked Creek and into Sunday Bay, and along Wilderness Waterway above the headwaters of the Huston River though Chevalier and Cannon Bays. You will paddle through the Chatham River—stopping by the infamous Watson Place—to the mouth of the Huston River and return to Everglades City along Gulf beaches, the shores of Duck Rock Cove, the Three Sisters, Pavilion Key, and Rabbit Key and across the mouth of Chokoloskee Pass into Sandfly Pass and then back into Chokoloskee Bay.

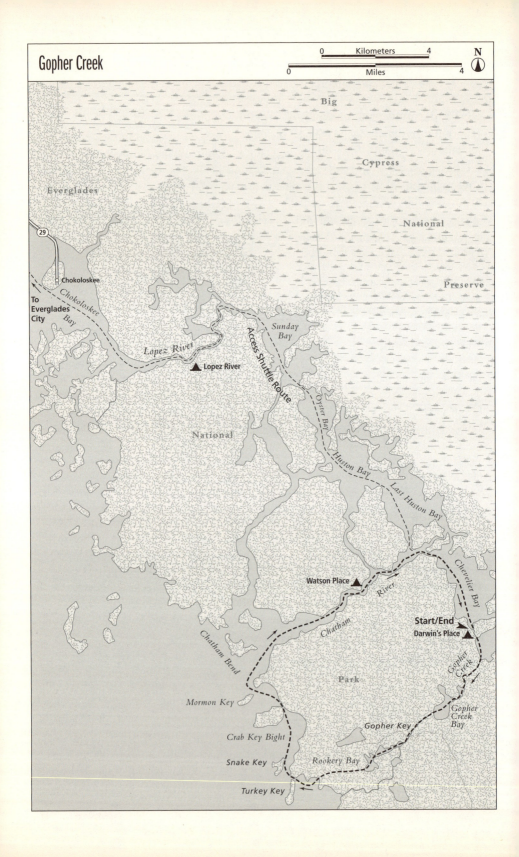

Gopher Creek offers the best wildlife photography available in the remote Everglades. Capt. Charlie Wright is located in Everglades City and I highly recommend him for photography, fishing and other guided tours.

You can paddle from campsite to campsite to get the whole Gopher Creek experience. But in order to truly explore the creek, you need to spend more than a night per campsite. For this trip, you can stay at the Watson Place one night and explore Sweetwater Bay. On your second day you can paddle 4.5 miles to Darwin's Place for a two-night stay. Place is located directly north and west of Darwin's Place, 4.5 miles, from the mouth of Gopher Creek, which runs from Cannon Bay.

To see where these campsites are in relation to Everglades City, go to the section for wilderness camping on the Everglades National Park Web site: www.nps.gov/archive/ever/visit/backcoun.htm.

Leave the Darwin's Place campsite and paddle south to Cannon Bay, staying along the west shore. You will pass a few small islands before reaching Gopher Creek. The first 0.3 mile of Gopher Creek is canopied by red and black mangroves, followed by an open area where the mangroves are shorter. The creek is open as you pass mud banks littered with dead tree trunks. This is where you'll see the most wildlife, which is easier to spot along the creek. You may also see gumbo-limbo trees in the background. The creek is about 50 feet wide and then narrows to about 30 feet across.

Gopher Creek continues like this for about 0.75 mile before opening up into Gopher Creek Bay. The bay is fairly long, about 0.5 mile, and then narrows and continues another 1.5 miles as a creek. Not too far away is Gopher Key, where you'll find a Calusa Indian shell mound. There really isn't any place to get out of your canoe or kayak, though—the mangroves have pretty much grown over the area.

Continuing toward the Gulf, paddling west-southwest, you eventually turn into a longer stretch of open water, Rookery Bay. The bay is about 1.5 miles from end to end and is spotted with several mangrove islands. At the Gulf end of the bay is a 2.0-mile-long creek that continues into the open Gulf. The only time one can get through here is during November and December, when the water levels are highest.

Hurricane Andrew in 1992 was not kind to the Gopher Creek area. As a result, the mangroves here are younger and smaller and there are many standing or downed dead tree trunks scattered about the entire creek area. The bays and creeks are a veritable fish soup. If you don't notice the fish, you'll notice the birds feeding on them. You won't see many alligators here, as the water is a bit salty for them, but a 3-foot-long shark was spotted in the creek not far from Cannon Bay.

One issue facing the Everglades is rising sea levels, which push more salinity into the marsh and mangrove wetlands. Together, hurricanes and the rising sea levels make this an ever-changing environment.

We had three days to explore Gopher Creek with our canoes. On one day we had enough time to paddle through Rookery Bay but no farther due to lack of water. The good part about shallow water is that it makes photographing wildlife much easier. The bad part is that shallow water makes it easier to get stuck (not a major problem in a canoe). The mud is like quicksand, so you never want to step out of your boat into the mud. We did find a couple of high spots where we could actually get out, but they are few and far between.

A canoe is much more convenient back in here. You don't want a situation where you have no choice but to get out of your boat to take care of business, which is pretty much the case with a kayak. In addition, photographing is much easier from a canoe because your gear is in the open and more easily accessed. I keep my camera in a dry bag in front of my seat so that I can grab it easily. Because I'm going slowly, not paddling great distances, and in an area protected from winds, I keep my camera on top of the bag. Another advantage of a canoe is you can set up a tripod more easily than in a kayak.

Many people, especially fishermen, go into Gopher Creek with a motorboat. The advantage of a motorboat is that you can cover more territory in less time. But you'll see and hear far more exploring by canoe. In a canoe you can actually *hear* the Everglades. You can drift along the creek slowly, stopping wherever you like to just sit and look, listen, and take it all in. A silent, stealthy approach does not scare wildlife as easily, although I am convinced that birds might think a slow, quiet canoe is a predator, because they do respond with some caution.

On one trip I spotted several juvenile birds, including blue herons, ibis, and anhingas. I saw so many tricolor herons that I lost count. I spotted an osprey having a fish for lunch, some brown pelicans in the bays, white pelicans flying overhead, and lots and lots of ibis. I found a small hidden mud bank with a snowy egret, juvenile little blue heron, juvenile white ibis, and an adult white ibis all feeding within a 5-foot radius. In the afternoon and early morning, I spotted several raccoons hunting for food along the creek. I followed one boar coon (about the size of a coyote) about 0.25 mile along the creek.

Return to Darwin's Place campsite, retracing your route, paddling east-northeast through Rookery Bay back toward Gopher Key through the creek. Remember that Gopher creek is wider and shallower here and will become deeper as you get closer to Cannon Bay. As you may recall, when you get to Cannon Bay, you are only 0.5 mile from Darwin's Place. Turn left and paddle north back to the campsite. You should see gumbo-limbo trees over the mangroves.

12 Indian Key Pass to Picnic Key

This paddle will take you near numerous mangrove islands. You will want to keep a chart and compass handy and be sure to check the tide before heading out. Birds and other wildlife can be sighted along the mangroves that flank your canoe or kayak along this paddle.

County: Collier (Ten Thousand Islands)
Start/End: Gulf Coast Ranger Station
Distance: 14.0 miles round-trip
Approximate float time: 4 to 6 hours (8+ hours, longer depending upon stay/camping)
Difficulty: Moderate paddling
Nearest town: Everglades City
Season: Fall and winter
Fees: Launch fee at Park Service ramp, payable at the ranger station
Highlights: Dolphins, birds
Hazards: Powerboats and commercial fishing boats

Campsites: Tiger Key, Picnic Keys, Kingston Key Chickee
Connectors: West Pass, Pavilion Key, Sandfly Island, Rabbit Key, Halfway Creek Canoe Trail, the Causeway
Getting there: From the junction of US 41 (Tamiami Trail) and FL 29, take FL 29 south into Everglades City. Continue through town and down to the Gulf Coast Ranger Station in Everglades National Park. The launch ramp is behind the ranger station.

The Paddle

Launch from the ranger station canoe ramp and head west across Chokoloskee Bay. (Be sure to check the tides before embarking.) You will see markers that connect

Throughout the Ten Thousand Islands you will come across many shorebirds like these pelicans; this is Comer's Key or Pelican Key.

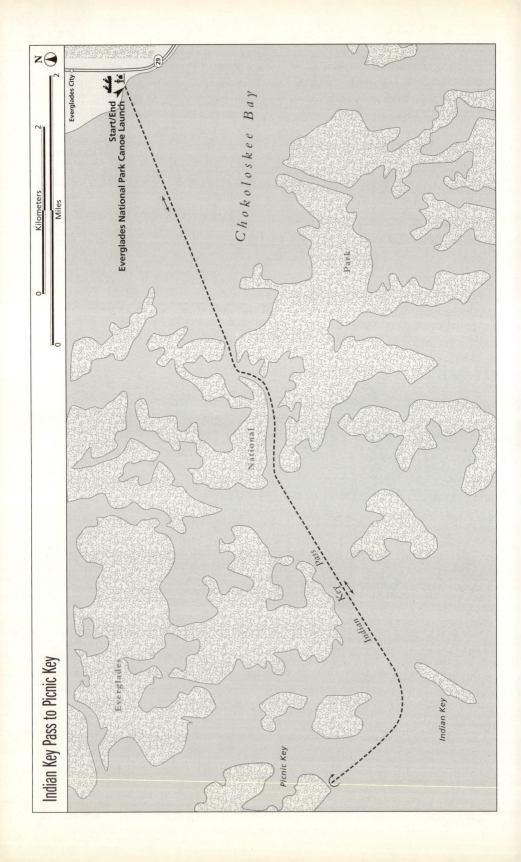

the Barron River to Sandfly Pass. Keep heading west toward Indian Key Pass while keeping an eye out for the boats that will be coming at you from various directions, including from the mouth of the Barron River. Mangrove islands of various sizes will flank either side of you.

After paddling about 1.5 miles, you will intersect Indian Key Pass at Marker 24. Enter Indian Key Pass where a sign says WELCOME TO THE EVERGLADES NATIONAL PARK. Some of the islands here may have dry land where you can stop, but most consist only of tangled mangrove props. As you paddle around, you will understand why this area is called Ten Thousand Islands.

At one time this area was dredged to admit larger vessels. Continue paddling west through the labyrinth of mangrove islands. The waterway widens and turns slightly south at Marker 15. As you continue your trek southwest, you will no doubt encounter tour boats and other powerboats, as this is a popular route to access several keys and campsites. At 3.5 miles, Marker 10, you will see the Gulf in front of you. Aim for Marker 6 and maneuver around the mangroves to Gaskin Bay. Continue paddling through the pass toward Indian Key and then northwest after the Stop Keys. Watch for the shallow water as you head for Kingston Key Chickee. Look for the beach area on the southwest side of Picnic Key. This is 7 miles and is a scenic island, great for picnicking or to camp for the night.

Return the same way you came in.

13 Tiger Key

This is a trip worth repeating, as you will likely see more the second or third trip out. On this relatively easy paddle, you can enter a quiet cove to discover roseate spoonbills nesting and teaching their young. You will more than likely encounter other resident birds, dolphins, and sea turtles. In spring you will paddle among dolphins and loggerhead turtles almost every day. The turtles will be hitting the beaches to lay eggs. They have moved nearer to shore recently, so you will see them regularly. By late April, early May, the migratory birds are heading north. However, the smaller birds crossing the Florida Straits will stop on the oyster bars for respite and repast.

With a permit, paddlers can overnight on the beach at either Picnic or Tiger Key. (Permits can be obtained at the Gulf Coast Visitor Center no more than twenty-four hours prior to your trip.) You can also fish along Tiger Key for snook and sea trout. Explore the tidal pools for crabs, sea stars, and other crustaceans.

County: Collier (Ten Thousand Islands)
Start/End: City Seafood (Everglades City) or Everglades National Park ramp
Distance: 16.0 miles round-trip
Approximate float time: Approximately 12 hours
Difficulty: Moderate paddling
Nearest town: Everglades City

Season: Fall, winter, and early spring
Fees: Launch fee at either boat ramp
Highlights: Nesting birds, usually roseate spoonbills, in cove; possibly ospreys, hawks, and dolphins; beaches; small area for picnicking
Hazards: Tides, currents, wind and powerboats

Getting there: From the junction of US 41 (Tamiami Trail) and FL 29, follow FL 29 south for 3 miles into Everglades City. Launch from the ramp at City Seafood (702 Begonia St., Everglades City) or from the National Park Service ramp behind the Gulf Coast Ranger Station (one mile south of City Seafood).

The Paddle

Launching from the Park Service ramp, head west and skirt to the right of a little island near the channel markers for Indian Key Pass. As you cross Chokoloskee Bay, you will encounter powerboat traffic as you pass through the channels of Sandfly Pass and Indian Key. Keep an eye to your right, toward the airport, where you may see bald eagles.

Paddle west with Bear Island on your right. A channel marker designates the mouth of the Barron River (0.75 mile from the ramp). Lane Cove, with mangroves islets, is on your left. Continue westward.

Tiger Key is a comfortable beach area and popular among boaters and paddlers. It's also great for shell surfing.

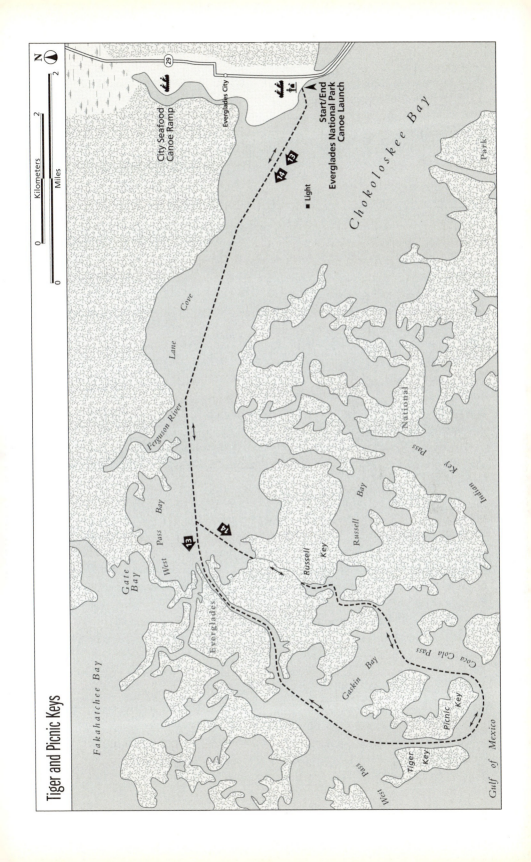

Chokoloskee Bay merges with Lane Cove on your right about 1.5 miles from the ramp. Keep paddling west, with the mainland on your right. Continue paddling another 1.5 miles along the mainland, which will provide a buffer from the wind if the wind is blowing from the north or northwest. There are jumping mullet in this area. You will come to a point that marks the end of Lane Cove and the entrance of the Ferguson River, 3.5 miles from the boat ramp. Lane Cove is a great place for fishing.

The mouth of the Ferguson River is sprinkled with mangrove islands and oyster bars. Continue paddling west, about 1.0 mile, to West Pass Bay. You won't see any channel markers; however, you should be able to follow the channel as it narrows. Depending on the time of year and time of day, you may see myriad birds in this area, including pelicans, swallow-tailed kites, and roseate spoonbills. This is a popular rookery.

You will come to a confluence of West Pass and the draining area of Gate and Fakahatchee Bays about 1.0 mile farther. Continue paddling around the mangroves to Tiger Key, on the west side, about 8.0 miles from the canoe ramp. There is a nice sandy beach on the northern side of the island where you can stop, stretch, picnic, and possibly camp. The western side has mangroves and mudflats. The mudflats are a great area for shell surfing: horseshoe crabs and other crustaceans. Look for their burrows in the sand and as they scurry across the shore. On a recent visit, a clothesline was hung between the trees where campers or picnickers dried their clothes in the warm ocean breeze.

According to our guide, some of the key's oyster beds have been lost because of runoff from pesticides and other lawn treatments for developments in and around south Florida.

When you are ready to leave, paddle around the east side of the island, with the shore on your left side. There's another small mangrove island on your right. You will see a bay on your left as you come through the pass. Paddle northeast and pass the north shore of Picnic Key. This is a great place to quietly enter the bay and watch roseate spoonbills hanging around in the trees or foraging for food. The juveniles will be camouflaged on the ground or in shallow muddy flats as they skim for their supper.

Cross Gaskin Bay and paddle through a channel past the Calusa Indian shell mounds on the west side of Russell Key. You will eventually circle 1.0 mile around this key. Follow this pass northeast and then curve north. A lake will open up on your left. Change direction and go right, into another lake. Continue paddling a few hundred feet and then bend sharply to your left, following the pass. Head north and northwest, meandering northwest by Russell Key. The shell mounds are now on your right in the mangroves. Mangrove grottos lead away from you on the right. This secluded area is usually quiet as well as attractive with little or no motorboat traffic. Listen for the prairie warblers and survey the area for other signs of wildlife. Continue to paddle along the shore on your left until you reach a point, and then head

Captain Laura takes paddlers into a secret rookery where roseate spoonbills, both juvenile and adult, can be found.

northeast. Keep an eye out for sandbars. Continue to West Pass, heading north and then into the bay. The radio tower near the airport is a good landmark.

Reversing direction going back in, head northeast and then east as you enter Lane Cove and then Chokoloskee Bay to the canoe ramp. Be aware of the wind, which can rise in the afternoon and cause waves to slosh over your canoe or kayak.

NOTE: This may not be the easiest or most direct route to navigate. You can also choose to go through Indian Key Pass.

14 Picnic Key

This is a great day or overnight trip (permit required) on either Picnic or Tiger Key. Tiger Key has great fishing for snook and sea trout. Take a break from paddling and explore the shorelines or shallow bays of both keys for sea anemones, starfish, and crabs and other crustaceans. West Pass, along the western border of the national park, may have less boat traffic than Indian, Sandfly, or Chokoloskee Pass. In Gaskin Bay and West Pass, dolphins may play and surf alongside you.

County: Collier (Ten Thousand Islands)
Start/End: Canoe ramp behind Everglades National Park headquarters building, Gulf Coast Ranger Station
Distance: Approximately 11 miles round-trip, depending on route taken
Difficulty: Easy to moderate paddling
Approximate float time: Approximately 6 to 7 hours
Nearest town: Everglades City
Season: Fall, winter, and early spring
Fees: Launch fee at canoe ramp, payable at the ranger station
Highlights: Beach 40 yards northeast of Tiger Key, camping area, ospreys and other birds, dolphins, bays
Hazards: Winds, powerboats, possible mud at launch site
Getting there: From the junction of US 41 (Tamiami Trail) and FL 29, follow FL 29 south for 3 miles into Everglades City and down to the Gulf Coast Ranger Station in Everglades National Park. The boat ramp is behind the ranger station.

The Paddle

Launch from the sand or muddy ramp behind the ranger station and head west. Paddle around to the right of a little island (Totch's Island) and cross through the channel and the markers. Keep an eye out for motorized boats in Chokoloskee Bay and in the Sandfly Connector or Indian Key Pass. Boats will be coming from your right, down the Barron River, and will be getting up on a plane, picking up speed and putting the boat up on the water, and they may not see smaller vessels in front of them. This is a good area for birding; bald eagles nest on the north side of the airport. Even after the hurricanes, within a year the migrating birds have returned to their habitat along the Washingtonian palms.

Bear Island is on your right as you paddle west. The mouth of the Barron River is about 0.75 mile from the canoe ramp. Continue paddling west, looking to your right for a channel marker for Lane Cove and to your left for a group of mangrove islands.

The bay merges with Lane Cove, 1.5 miles from the ramp, at the first major point from the mainland. Continue west, paddling between the oyster bars and the mangrove islets, with the mainland on your right. The mainland can minimize the wind if it is blowing strongly from the north or northwest.

From here paddle another 1.5 miles toward another point from the mainland, which marks the end of Lane Cove. Throughout Lane Cove you may happen upon strands of egrets or see cormorants flying overhead. Your paddling should be a journey, not a race to the camp or chickee. Take time to peer into the mangroves and watch egrets hop around, plundering for a meal. The jumping, or flying, fish are usually mullet. You can observe pelicans diving for mullet as you glide along.

The mouth of the Ferguson River, a small opening where several streams of water converge, lies 3.5 miles from the boat ramp. The shoreline consists of oyster bars and mangroves. Paddle west 1.0 mile across West Pass Bay to the mouth of West Pass, where the channel narrows. This channel is a great bird rookery, recognizable by the guano on the trees. You can see swallow-tailed kites over the tops of the mangroves as they hunt for arboreal lizards and frogs.

Picnic key is a popular place for boaters to hang out and camp. It's also a great place for shell surfing and picnicking.

In another 1.5 miles you will come to a merging of several streams where Gate and Fakahatchee Bays drain and meet up with West Pass Bay. Continue as though you were heading to Tiger Key. This popular beach and campsite area has eroded some over the years, but it is still a great place to stop and stretch your legs, shell surf, or picnic. On the west side of the island you can see the tracks of baby horseshoe crabs, shrimp burrows, and fiddler crabs waving their claws. The male crab has one claw larger than the other; the female's claws are the same size. Tiger Key is approximately 5.75 miles from your launch site.

As you pass around the northern tip of the island, paddle southeast and enter Coca Cola Pass, which runs between Tiger and Picnic Keys as well as on the eastern side of Picnic Key. Picnic Key, on your left, has a stunning beach on the south shore and possibly an outhouse. The south part of the island offers great fishing for sea trout, which you will find in the sea grass flats. You can pull up on the beach to stretch, picnic, or camp for the night (permit required). Explore this treasure trove of sea creatures, but keep an eye on the weather. The winds can be strong going around the island, and you will be paddling against the tide.

When you are ready to leave, paddle around the east side of the island, with the shore on your left side. There's another small mangrove island on your right. You will see a bay on your left as you come through the pass. Paddle northeast and pass the north shore of Picnic Key. This is a great place to quietly enter the bay and watch roseate spoonbills hanging around in the trees or foraging for food. The juveniles will be camouflaged on the ground or in shallow muddy flats as they skim for their supper.

Cross Gaskin Bay and paddle through a channel past the Calusa Indian shell mounds on the west side of Russell Key. You will eventually circle 1.0 mile around this key. Follow this pass northeast and then curve north. A lake will open up on your left. Change direction and go right, into another lake. Continue paddling a few hundred feet and then bend sharply to your left, following the pass. Head north and northwest, meandering northwest by Russell Key. The shell mounds are now on your right in the mangroves. Mangrove grottos lead away from you on the right. This secluded area is usually quiet as well as attractive, with little or no motorboat traffic. Listen for the prairie warblers and survey the area for other signs of wildlife. Continue to paddle along the shore on your left until you reach a point, and then head northwest. Keep an eye out for sandbars. Continue to West Pass, heading north and then into the bay. The radio tower near the airport is a good landmark.

Reversing direction going back in, head northeast and then east as you enter Lane Cove and then Chokoloskee Bay to the canoe ramp. Be aware of the wind, which can rise in the afternoon and cause waves to slosh over your canoe or kayak.

15 Jewell Key

This is a shorter day trip than Tiger or Picnic Key that offers great birding. Time your trip with the outgoing tide. This route can also be a little tricky on navigation. You will paddle past Sandfly Island and through Sandfly Pass, following channel markers as streams branch off to the sides. Once on Jewell Key you can enjoy a picnic and explore the island with its tidepools. Comer Key, off to northwest, is often covered with pelicans and other birds for viewing.

County: Collier (Ten Thousand Islands)
Start/End: Canoe ramp behind the Everglades National Park headquarters building, Gulf Coast Ranger Station
Distance: 12.0 miles round-trip
Approximate float time: Approximately 8 hours
Difficulty: Moderate paddling
Nearest town: Everglades City
Season: Fall, winter, and early spring

Fees: Launch fee at canoe ramp, payable at ranger station
Highlights: Beaches, bird rookery
Hazards: Wind, tides, motorized boats; muddy at launch site
Getting there: From the junction of US 41 (Tamiami Trail) and FL 29, follow FL 29 south for 3 miles into Everglades City and down to the Gulf Coast Visitor Center in Everglades National Park. The boat ramp is behind the ranger station.

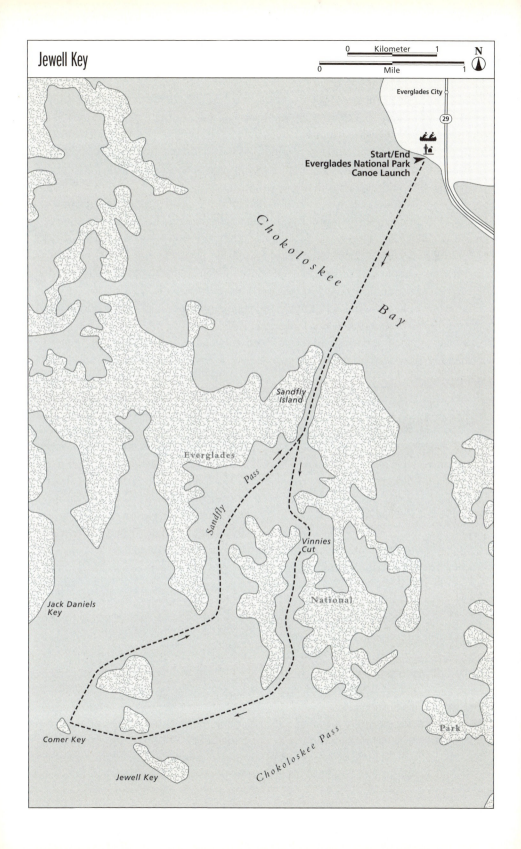

The Paddle

Launch from the ramp and paddle south toward Sandfly Pass and look for channel markers. You will be able to see the pass because of the boat traffic. Once in the channel, you will be able to see Sandfly Island, about 1.5 miles from the launch. There may still be an outhouse on the island (if it has not been blown away by storms). Sandfly Pass curves to the west. You may notice an osprey nest in the area. January through April, the birds are usually on the nest with eggs or chicks.

Just over 2.0 miles from the put-in, turn left into an unmarked pass (often referred to as Vinnie's Cut on maps) to Jewell Key. To your right, another channel leads to a beautiful bay and smaller creeks. Paddle southeast 160 degress between mangrove islands. After entering this pass, continue paddling southeast to a large bay with a mangrove island in the middle. Paddle around to the right of the island and stay on the pass.

After exiting Vinnie's Cut, you will see more trees either to the front or on your right, depending on where you came out. This is Jewell Key rookery. Continue paddling toward the island and you will see a beach. Dividing this beach is a cut that will take you to the Gulf of Mexico. Jewell Key's sandy beach offers a respite for picnicking, photography, or just stretching your legs. Be careful of the sharp oyster shells along the pit—you can easily cut yourself. This island also affords you a peek at the native life: horseshoe crabs, birds and more. During low tide, you can explore the shoreline. The west side has a more rocky terrain, mangroves, and tidal pools.

Looking from Jewell Key's sand pit to the northwest, out to sea, you will see a sandy beach—when it's not covered by a colossal flock of pelicans. During the winter months, you may not even be able to see the sand for the white pelicans, Forester's terns, black skimmers, American oystercatchers, sanderlings, willets, and other shorebirds. This is Comer Key, previously called Pelican Key and, before that, Bird Key. Older charts may show symbols for camping and trees. This is no longer true—there are no trees on the island, and it often disappears during high tide. Prior to Hurricane Donna in 1960, there was vegetation on the island and a shack owned by Robert Roy Osmer. The hurricane obliterated both building and vegetation, leaving a deserted island in its wake.

When you are ready to leave Jewell Key, paddle west from the cut toward Comer Key. Do not approach the birds, which may take flight or begin to walk around. Cormorants will often take off when anyone approaches the island. Most of these birds are migrating birds that will begin their spring migration north and therefore need to reserve their calories. The more active they are, the more they need to eat (there goes your fishing). Use binoculars or a camera with telephoto lens to get a closer view or take photos.

At this point you have a few options regarding which direction to paddle. Paddling north will take you around the western edge of two islands, with Jack Daniels Key on your left. Then you would paddle northeast toward Sandfly Pass. Or you can take a more direct route, heading east-northeast and heading through a pass between two unnamed islands north of Jewell Key. From here you would paddle north-northeast toward Sandfly Pass.

From here you can also choose to paddle northeast and then north through a narrow pass dividing two unnamed islands in front of you. The smaller island has nice views of red mangroves and wilderness along the shoreline. When you exit this cut through the mangroves, head north with Jack Daniels Key on your left and a few smaller islands ahead of you. Paddle to your right around a point and head east-northeast. Sandfly Pass is on your left. (There will be boat traffic in this pass.) If you head back through the pass when the tide is coming out, the tide will be strong and you will have to paddle harder to get through the mouth of Sandfly Pass to Chokoloskee Bay. Keep an eye out for commercial boats, which will be heading back to Everglades City along this route.

Sandfly Pass becomes fragmented as it comes into Chokoloskee Bay. It's best to select a side channel to avoid the rush of the current. You will be able to see the Gulf Coast Ranger Station from here. Paddle northeast to reach the canoe ramp.

16 Rabbit Key

This paddle offers a plethora of ecosystems. The mangroves you'll see from your kayak on this excursion can seem like cathedrals. Be sure to go out during high tide, when the oyster bars are covered. As you pass through the mangrove islands, you can see ospreys, yellow-crested hens and roseate spoonbills. Dolphins can also be seen frolicking among the groves. You may encounter muddy water when it's low tide. As you paddle between the islands, you will see shallow, sandy bottoms. Auger Hole, a well-known spot, is not marked on the maps. You'll know it by the oyster bar just before it. Auger Hole will take you to Rabbit Key Grasses; however, at times this route can be impassable.

County: Collier (Ten Thousand Islands)
Start/End: Chokoloskee Bay, from the causeway or Outdoor Resorts' boat ramp
Difficulty: Moderate to difficult paddling
Approximate float time: 6 to 7 hours
Distance: 8.0 miles round-trip
Nearest town: Everglades City
Season: Fall and winter
Fees: Possible launch fee at Outdoor Resorts' boat ramp

Highlights: Beaches, dolphins, turtles, osprey nest, unique passes
Hazards: Oyster bars, strong winds, tides, motorboats; difficult navigation
Getting there: From the junction of US 41 (Tamiami Trail) and FL 29, follow FL 29 south through Everglades City and down to Chokoloskee, about 7 miles. You can park along the causeway to launch or launch from the ramp at Outdoor Resorts (239-695-3788).

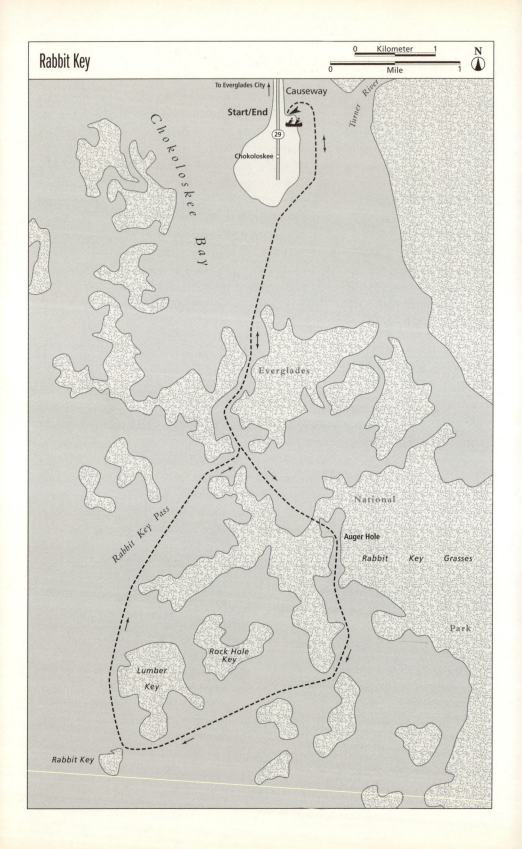

The Paddle

From the causeway paddle into the bay and head south along the shore of Chokoloskee Island. Be sure to check the tide charts before going out. At high tide the oyster bars will be covered. At high tide you will want to paddle south; at low tide you will need to paddle more to the east and then south around the shoals. Several passes will take you to Rabbit Key. Some of the easternmost passes have more boat traffic than others; however, they all eventually merge. Keep a chart and compass handy.

Look for the mangrove islands that are more pointed and distinctive, and head to this pass. Paddle around the small mangrove islands; from the split this pass heads southeast. To newcomers to the region, mangroves may appear monotonous. However, if you allow yourself to slow down and share the rhythm of nature, you may learn to appreciate them. One paddler said the "mangroves turn into cathedrals."

This is a usually peaceful area with a shallow, sandy bottom. Warblers may serenade here. As you pass through the islands, you may see other migrating and permanent residents, including ospreys, yellow-crested night herons, and roseate spoonbills.

Turn right to head toward the key. After exiting the pass, look for Rabbit Key (south). At this point you have paddled about 3.0 miles. There is a large sandbar at Rabbit Key. You can paddle around it or stop (at low tide) for a stretch and to take pictures. Inland you may find an active osprey nest during winter. One regular paddler in this area saw a manta ray blast out of the water in front of her kayak. Dolphins are common in this area, and birds find fishing plentiful. Every bird you see here will probably have a fish in its beak or talons.

Paddle south from the sandbar to the far end of the bay and Auger Hole, which is on your left. Auger Hole (not labeled on charts) is a creek that runs through the mangroves and can take you to Rabbit Key Grasses. Auger Hole is fronted by an oyster bar, which can be difficult, if not impossible, to navigate during low tide.

Paddle through Auger Hole to a small pond and head southeast into the bay. Head toward the shore lined with mangroves, about 0.25 mile away. The bay turns south and is muddy along the shore. A creek leads off to the east as the bay narrows and then opens to a larger bay—Rabbit Key Grasses.

Paddle south with the mainland on your right and follow around the tip. A network of islands will greet you, with Lumber and Rock Hole Keys on your right. From here you will paddle about 1.25 miles west to reach Rabbit Key, and you will need to turn about 250 degrees to your right. Along the way you may see dolphins frolicking about. As you paddle west past Lumber Key, you should be able to see the beach of Rabbit Key ahead. There is a large sandbar between Lumber and Rabbit Keys. During high tide, boats won't see the sandbar. Rabbit Key is a great area for picnicking and exploring the island and its inhabitants. You can also camp here for the night with a permit. There is even an outhouse on this island.

To return to Chokoloskee, paddle north from Rabbit Key about 350 degrees past the northwest tip of Lumber Key, and then continue north past Turtle Key. Keep a watchful eye for sea turtles lazily swimming around the island. As you pass this island, keep just south of Rabbit Key Pass, watching for powerboats. Continue on a northeast course, with a few small islands on your left. Paddle through the pass; it will narrow and turn to the east about one mile from Turtle Key. The pass will turn sharply toward the north and the mainland (a heading of about 80 degrees). You will come to the marker you passed on the way out. After exiting the pass, Chokoloskee should be visible to the north. Continue paddling toward the island with Chokoloskee on your left as you enter back around the tip to your start/end.

17 Last Huston Bay Route

This route will take you south on the Wilderness Waterway—a 99-mile waterway from Flamingo to Everglades City. This paddle is "inside" the Everglades, as opposed to being out in the bay or Gulf with open water littered with islands. Enveloped by mangrove trees, this easy paddle takes you through a course marked with channel markers. You will paddle down the Wilderness Waterway around a few small islands, one with a home on stilts. You should see a variety of birds along this route.

County: Collier (Ten Thousand Islands)
Start: Sunday Bay Chickee; shuttle from Everglades City
End: Chatham River, Wilderness Waterway Marker 99
Distance: 7.0 miles one-way
Approximate float time: 5 hours
Difficulty: Mild to moderate paddling
Nearest town: Everglades City
Season: Fall and winter
Fees: None at Sunday Bay Chickee; shuttle fee
Highlights: Birding, Wilderness Waterway
Hazards: Powerboats on Wilderness Waterway
Campsites: Sunday Bay Chickee, Watson Place

Connectors: Hurdles Creek, Huston River, Chatham River, Darwin's Place
Getting there: From the intersection of US 41 (Tamiami Trail) and FL 29, follow FL 29 south for 3 miles into Everglades City and down to the Gulf Coast Ranger Station. The boat ramp is behind the ranger station. Due to the distance, you will want to arrange a shuttle to take you to Sunday Bay Chickee. This can be accessed via the Lopez River. Many powerboats will access this route for fishing. This route is east of the Rock Hole and Lumber Keys and Rabbit Key Pass.

The Paddle

This route is on the inside of the mangrove islands and bays as you paddle southeast on the Wilderness Waterway. Winds can pick up on the bay, as can tides, especially with more powerboat traffic on the waterway, causing some waves as you paddle inside the bays or small lakes within the mangroves.

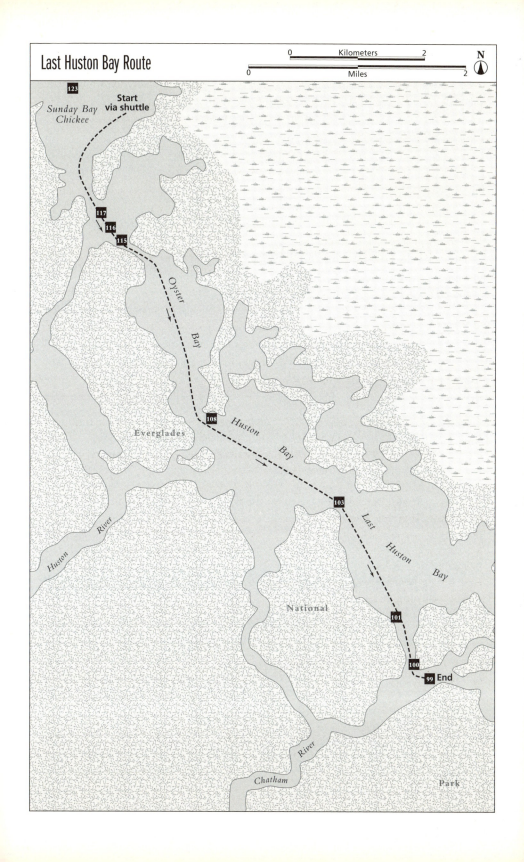

Launch from Sunday Bay Chickee and head to Marker 123, which is just west of Sunday Bay Chickee on the Wilderness Waterway. You will be paddling south down the Wilderness Waterway to the end of the bay, following the markers in descending numerical order as you paddle between several islands.

The Huston River is a channel south of two small islands. Pass through this channel into an open bay. Continue on through Marker 117 and then Marker 116, between two more islands. You will need to turn south again to find Marker 115. These two markers (115 and 116) are relatively close together. Oyster Bay lies ahead in a southeasterly direction. Continue paddling across this bay, passing several small islands as the marker numbers continue to decrease. Huston Bay opens up at Marker 108. You have traveled 3.0 miles from the chickee.

From here paddle toward a home built on an island near Marker 107. Go along the east shore of this island, heading toward the pass at the southeast of Huston Bay—Marker 103 on the Wilderness Waterway. Just past this marker is Last Huston Bay. Both Huston and Last Huston Bays tend to be relatively shallow, about 2 to 4 feet deep. Mangroves circle the lake, Last Huston Bay.

Paddle to the south corner of Last Huston Bay. Look for Marker 101 and then head into the channel. This waterway splits at Marker 100. The channel to the right (west) will take you to Chatham River. For this route continue on the left (east) channel. At Marker 99 you have paddled about 7.0 miles since you launched from the Sunday Bay Chickee. This is your take-out point, or you can follow one of the other options. Power boats will also be coming through the Chatham River. You can arrange for a shuttle to pick you up here.

Options: You will intersect the Chatham River Route. Watson Place is only 1.5 miles southwest down the Chatham River. Sweetwater Chickee is 2.0 miles northeast. The Darwin's Place route starts here and meanders southeast 9.5 miles down the Wilderness Waterway to Lostman's Five campsite.

18 A Scenic Mangrove Tunnel on the Wilderness Waterway

On this all-day paddle you will head out from town and travel through a scenic mangrove tunnel. Along the way you should spot dolphins and other wildlife living it up. From town you will paddle past a historic trading post and museum (now the Smallwood Store) and along the tip of Chokoloskee Island. You want to keep an eye out for oyster bars along the way. Look for the red and black mangroves a few miles out. When this route splinters off, maintain a heading south to enjoy the crustaceans and cover from the sun.

County: Collier (Ten Thousand Islands)
Start/End: Chokoloskee Causeway or Outdoor Resorts
Distance: Approximately 9.0 miles round-trip
Approximate float time: 5+ hours round-trip
Difficulty: Moderate paddling
Nearest town: Everglades City
Season: Fall and winter
Fees: Possible launch fee at Outdoor Resorts' boat ramp

Highlights: Mangrove tunnel, bays, dolphins, and other wildlife
Hazards: Wind, tides, oyster bars, powerboats; risky navigation
Getting there: From the intersection of US 41 (Tamiami Trail) and FL 29, follow FL 29 south Everglades City and down through to Chokoloskee, about 7 miles. You can park along the causeway to launch or launch from the ramp at Outdoor Resorts, possible fee (239-695-3788).

The Paddle

Launch from the northeastern point of Chokoloskee Island and paddle southwest and then keeping the island on your left, continue southeast toward the southern tip of Chokoloskee Island. If you paddle on the east side, you will pass the Smallwood Store, a historic trading post and museum. From this point continue paddling southeast toward the Wilderness Waterway. Watch for oyster bars at low tide. From the Outdoor Resort canoe ramp, you'll be paddling along the west side of the island, heading southwest then southeast toward the waterway. Follow the Wilderness Waterway to the Lopez River, however we are not going into the Lopez.

Watch for shoals as you paddle toward the Lopez River. You will also see markers for Rabbit Key Pass. As you pass Rabbit Key, you will see mangroves on the western shoreline. Head toward the mangroves and then turn south into a bay, with the mangroves on your right. The entrance to the mangrove tunnel is on the edge of the bay. To the east is the Lopez River, 3.5 miles from the launch site.

As you enter the tunnel of both red and black mangroves, you are heading south with a nice current. The tunnel is a nice reprieve from the sun and possible motorboats zipping by. This mangrove tunnel may be alive with wildlife—from snails and crabs to occasional birds foraging for their next meal. Smaller creeks flow off to your left and then rejoin the main channel you are on.

Continue paddling through the tunnel. Less than 1.0 mile into the tunnel, you will come to a small island that you will need to paddle around. The west side may be the easier paddle. Maintain your heading south again in the channel.

The channel splits a little farther down. Continuing south will take you to Rabbit Key Grasses. Turn right and head northwest under a mangrove arch and into a lake. You can paddle on either the east or west shore of this shallow lake to exit for Rabbit Key Pass. The tide or water level will determine which side of the lake to follow. When the water is high enough, paddling the east shore and then northwest across the lake and into Rabbit Key Pass is a better ride.

Continue paddling north, and then follow the shore, heading east for a while. Look for a creek on your left, and turn in here. This creek alternately widens and

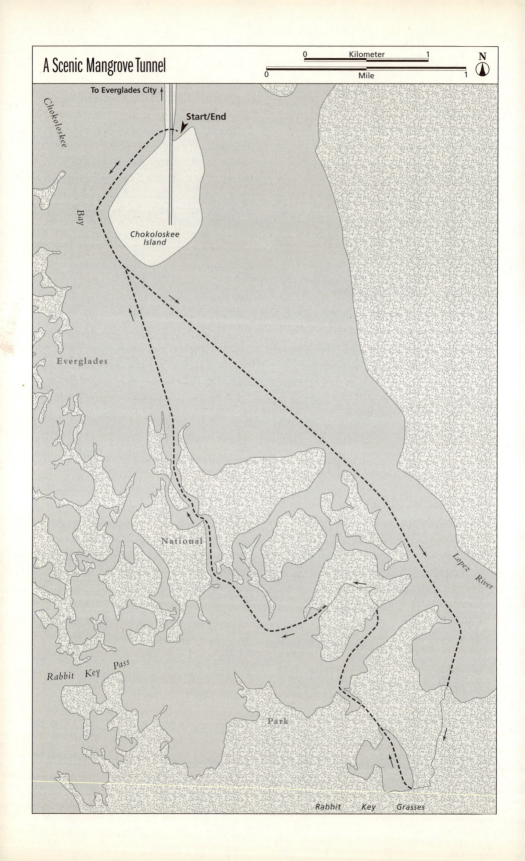

narrows before opening up into a bay. Again turn left to enter Rabbit Key Pass and follow this waterway. Just before the end of the creek is a small island you need to paddle around. There should be a channel marker here. Turn and head northwest for about 0.5 mile before reaching another pass that will take you back to Chokoloskee Bay. (**NOTE:** Several other passes leading north or northwest can take you back to the bay.)

The suggested pass widens after it turns north, and you will come across another small island to paddle around. Try to stay to the right as you pass this islet. You will turn west and then northwest as you press on. When you reach the bay, look across the water toward Chokoloskee Island and head back toward your launch site.

19 Chatham River Route

This is a nice paddle up the Chatham River, along the mangroves and shallow bars. You will need to pay attention to some navigation along the way, or you will find yourself heading up the Huston River instead. You may see flocks of ibis and pods of dolphins along the way. You will pass concrete pilings from an old bridge and paddle past Watson Place, an old homestead about 4.0 miles from Mormon Key. This used to be a successful cane farm and you may still see some old farm equipment.

County: Collier (Ten Thousand Islands)
Start: Mormon Key (shuttle from ENP or City Seafood boat ramp or Chokoloskee)
End: Sweetwater Chickee
Distance: 7.5 miles one-way
Approximate float time: 4 to 5 hours
Difficulty: Moderate paddling
Nearest town: Everglades City
Season: Fall, winter, and early spring
Fees: Launch fee at boat ramp
Highlights: Old homesite
Hazards: Watson Place ghost, sand and mud bars; some challenges in navigation and tide
Campsites: Mormon Key, Watson Place, Sweetwater Chickee

Connectors: Pavilion Key, Turkey Key, Last Huston Bay, Huston River, Darwin's Place
Getting there: From the intersection of US 41 (Tamiami Trail) and FL 29, follow FL 29 south for 3 miles into Everglades City and down to the Gulf Coast Ranger Station. The boat ramp is behind the Everglades National Park headquarters building. You can either paddle out to Mormon Key or get a lift from a powerboat to shorten the trip. Or, you can drive 7 miles from FL 29 and US 41, south through Everglades City, down to Chokoloskee Causeway. Park along the road to unload and use boat ramp. Keep in mind this will add several hours and miles to your paddle trip.

The Paddle

Take a shuttle from the ENP or City Seafood boat ramp out to Mormon Key, approximately 7 to 8 miles further southeast from Rabbit Key. From Chokoloskee Causeway boat ramp, you would have to paddle southeast around the mangroves and islands. You

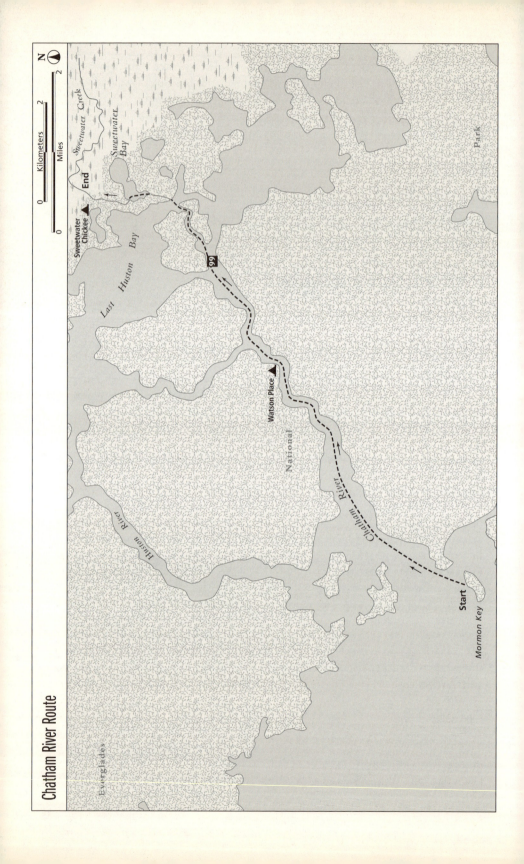

A small beach area to dock your canoe or kayak at Watson Place.

can maneuver through these islands down past Rabbit Key, which would be on your right bearing southeast toward Pavilion Key, one of the larger, outer islands and also a campsite. This will be open water and you will pass a smaller island, Dog Key, on your left, same side as the mainland. Heading due south you should see Mormon Island, also a great campsite. Mormon Island is about 4 to 5 miles south of Pavilion Key.

Launch from Mormon Key and paddle north toward the mouth of the Chatham River. Be careful you don't paddle too far to the west, or you might find yourself heading up the Huston River. You will encounter some shallow areas as you head upriver. The river is about 60 feet wide, sometimes wider, and the channel gets deeper as you come across some islands in the river delta.

Paddle northeast between oyster bars and mudflats along the mangrove-lined shores. You may see some pickerelweed interspersed among the mangroves. Take this route from the lower Ten Thousand Islands into the interior of the Glades. Flocks of ibis and pods of dolphins have been known to voyage through these waters. Along the way you will also see smaller streams leading into the river.

Weave your way around the bends—this should help break up the wind and current you will encounter along the way. Continue paddling. You will see the pilings and concrete of an old dock on the south shore, as well as some dry land. As you paddle around another bend, you will come across a water-monitoring station on the opposite shore (north). You have arrived at the infamous Watson Place campsite, 4.0 miles from your Mormon Key launch site. There is a dock here, and tourist, or gumbo-limbo, trees tower over the old homesite. This parcel of thirty-five to forty acres was once a successful cane and vegetable farm. Today the homesite consists of a cistern, old farm equipment, and a brick enclosure. Other remnants of the former homesite lie in the woods. This is a popular place for camping, picnicking, exploring—and telling ghost stories about "Emperor" Watson and his alleged victims (see sidebar).

Today the island's only inhabitants are likely to be a family of raccoons, opossums, birds, or maybe even an alligator. Feel free to fish from the dock for your next meal. Dolphins and birds such as hawks and herons may be your companions.

As you launch from Watson Place, you may see shells along the shore. Paddle north and west where gumbo-limbo trees line the shore. The Chatham River expands when it meets up with an unnamed creek, which takes you to Huston Bay. Stay on the river, which continues easterly and then heads north again. You will paddle past a few islands on your journey toward the Wilderness Waterway. By the time you reach Marker 99, you have gone 5.5 miles. Continuing 7.0 miles to the northwest, up Last Huston Bay, will take you to Sunday Bay Chickee. Darwin's Place is 3.0 miles southeast.

Our route leads up the Chatham River, heading east toward Sweetwater Bay and to the chickee. The river is wide at this point—70-plus feet. As you continue paddling up this channel, you will come to another route to Last Huston Bay. Since Sweetwater Chickee cannot be accessed from Last Huston Bay, you do not want to paddle into the bay. Instead, from the channel paddle northeast about 200 feet to an opening along the shore. This is the mouth of Sweetwater Creek. Head north as the river expands to about 40 feet across, paddling past Sweetwater Bay on your right. Continue on this route until you see a rather large island with palm trees. The chickee is on the opposite side of this island.

You are 2.0 miles from Wilderness Waterway and 7.5 miles from Mormon Key.

"EMPEROR" WATSON

Rumor has it that Edgar J. Watson came to the glades in the late 1800s and settled in Chatham Bend. He purchased the claim to the Old Calusa mound on the Chatham River from the widow of the previous owner, who was a fugitive and had been killed. A successful farmer and entrepreneur, Watson was dubbed "Emperor" Watson because of his grand schemes to develop the southwest of Florida.

It is noted that Watson didn't like anyone standing in his way, often reacting violently if anyone did. Before coming to the Everglades, Watson had been charged with the murder of Belle Starr, the "Outlaw Queen." However, the case didn't make it to trial because there was not enough evidence.

In the Everglades Watson was under suspicion for several incidents, including one where a man was injured and two men were killed. Drifters and the like often would stop to work on Watson's farm. Farmhands mysteriously disappeared, especially on payday, and in the early 1900s workers from the farm were discovered floating in the Chatham River with weights attached to their bodies.

People living nearby on Chokoloskee Island became concerned and then enraged. When Watson was held responsible for these deaths, he tried to convince the townspeople that his foreman, Leslie Cox, was responsible and that he would deliver him to the law. When all Watson delivered was a hat with a bullet hole in it, his neighbors were displeased.

When Watson landed on Chokoloskee on October 24, 1910, in an attempt to explain the death of his workers, his neighbors gunned him down near the Smallwood Store.

20 Darwin's Place

NOTE: Darwin's Place campsite has been closed due to vandalism. Check with a park ranger as to current use and availability.

This route offers several historic venues and scenic waterways and you will paddle through Chevelier Bay. Jean Chevelier, a Frenchman, supposedly collected and stuffed birds while also pluming in the area in the late 1800s. It is rumored that he buried some treasure here. As you paddle south you will be heading down the Wilderness Waterway. In about three miles you will arrive at Darwin's Place, an old shell mound, where you can stretch your legs. Darwin is said to have been the last living person in this area, which dates back to the Calusa Indians. You will see a variety of fauna and flora along this route, including gumbo-limbo and buttonwood trees.

County: Collier (Ten Thousand Islands)
Start: Marker 99, Wilderness Waterway
End: Lostman's Five campsite
Distance: 9.5 miles one-way (from Chokoloskee to Marker 99 it's an additional 16 miles)
Approximate Float Time: 5+ hours for Marker 99 to Lostman's Five campsite; additional 5+ hours from Chokoloskee
Difficulty: Mild paddling
Nearest town: Everglades City
Season: Fall and winter
Fees: Launch fee at boat ramp
Highlights: Shell mounds, vegetation
Hazards: Powerboats, wind, shallow water

Campsites: Darwin's Place, Plate Creek, Lostman's Five
Connectors: Last Huston Bay, Chatham River, Gopher Key, Willy Willy Route
Getting there: From the intersection of US 41 (Tamiami Trail) and FL 29, follow FL 29 south for 3 miles into Everglades City and down to the Gulf Coast Ranger Station. The boat ramp is behind the ranger station. From here you can paddle all the way out, which would be approximately another 16 additional miles and 5+ additional hours. Or you can hire a shuttle if you wish to save time.

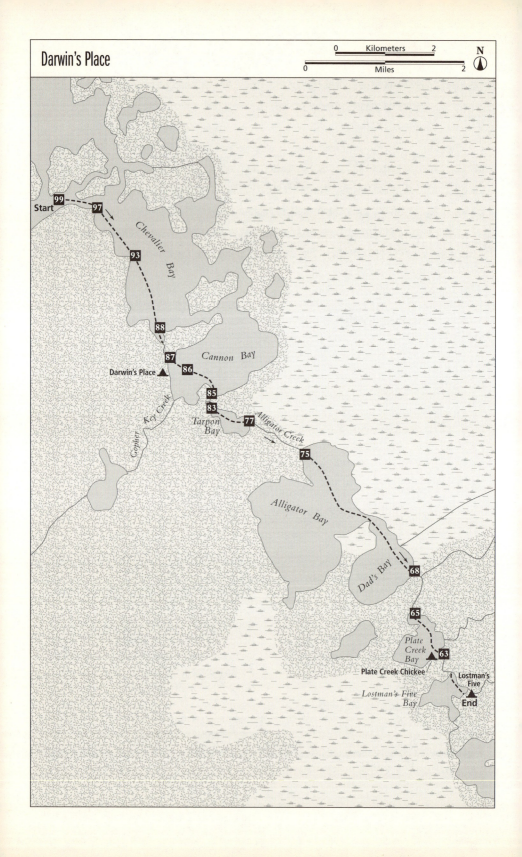

The Paddle

Begin your trek on the Wilderness Waterway at Marker 99, where the Chatham River meets the waterway, and paddle east toward Chevelier Bay. As you paddle around the point here, at Marker 97, the water will probably be shallow. This bay was named for Frenchman Jean Chevelier, who collected and stuffed birds while also pluming in and around the area of Opossum Key in the late 1800s. Rumor has it that he buried treasure somewhere in the Everglades. People have searched nearby islands for years looking for his cache.

Continue paddling in the bay, along the south shore. Mangroves border the waterway as you begin to turn and head south. As you head into the Wilderness Waterway, you will pass Marker 93 and head toward a passage near a single island. Follow the shoreline to Marker 88. You will soon come to a small creek; enter here. Paddle south again, to Marker 87. Continue paddling until you arrive at Darwin's Place, 3.0 miles from Marker 99.

Arthur Darwin was the last resident of an area that dates back to the Calusa Indians. The shell mound at the campsite is overgrown now; however, in the past the mound has had houses and crops on it. This is a good place to stretch, explore, and camp. (Check with a park ranger on camping availability before heading out.)

Paddle southeast from Darwin's Place and continue past Markers 86 and 85, heading toward some islands. To the east is Cannon Bay; to the southwest is the opening to Gopher Key Creek. Stay on the waterway, following a narrow creek south into Tarpon Bay. (This isn't the Tarpon Bay by the Harney River.) Continue paddling through this bay until you come to Alligator Creek, identified by Marker 77. This is one of two waterways in the Everglades named Alligator Creek. The other Alligator Creek is located on the West Lake Canoe Trail. The creek meanders a little bit before heading almost straight, southeast toward the large Alligator Bay.

As you paddle into the creek, you traverse a deep channel through tall mangroves. You may also see palm and buttonwood trees. The creek alternately widens and narrows again until you reach Alligator Bay at Marker 75. Alligator Bay, 1.0 mile across, supports palms and wax myrtles.

Paddle southeast toward a channel that will connect you to Dad's Bay. On your right (southwest) is the vastness of Alligator Bay. Go around a point and enter Dad's Bay. You now have paddled about 6.0 miles. Like the lake before, the bulkiness of Dad's Bay is on the southwest. Along the east shore you may notice a small canal, Gator Bay, perhaps the remnants of former attempts to drain the lake for development.

Continue paddling along Dad's Bay until you come to Maker 68 on the east side. From here you will enter the "no wake" zone into Plate Creek, which got its name when Gregorio Lopez dropped a plate into the water. A Mexican novelist and journalist, Lopez was also one of the leading chroniclers of the Mexican Revolution. The shores along this creek are littered with palm, buttonwood, coco plum, and poisonwood trees.

Plate Creek begins at Marker 65. From here you can see the chickee on an island not far ahead (8.5 miles from your launch site, Marker 99). On the north side another canal leads away from the bay. This goes a little ways up before you are unable to paddle any farther due to overgrown vegetation.

Plate Creek Chickee was built on the remnants of an old building and parts of the shelter were constructed from the old water tower. This is a scenic place to rest, camp, or just enjoy the quiet with palm trees and mangroves encircling you.

As you leave the chickee, you will come to an inlet and another creek (Marker 63.). Lostman's Five Bay is a short distance away. The campsite is across the bay, southeast toward the mouth of Lostman's Five Creek (9.5 miles from your launch site at Marker 99).

Options: It's another 8.0 miles on the Willy Willy and Lostman's River routes to the Gulf of Mexico and 10.0 miles to Willy Willy campsite using the Willy Willy route.

Cape Sable, Whitewater Bay, and Flamingo

21 Big Sable Route

This route can be challenging with the winds and tides from the open ocean, the river, and the bay. This is a full-day paddle. You won't find any dry land on which to stop and picnic, but you can tie up to a tree to each lunch and wade to stretch your legs. This wonderful route gives you a good view of the ecosystem both inside and outside the Everglades, the Gulf of Mexico, and another habitat.

County: Collier (Ten Thousand Islands)
Start: Beach at Northwest Cape
End: Oyster Bay Chickee
Distance: 13.0 miles one-way (from Flamingo to Northwest Cape, add approximately 20 miles)
Approximate float time: 6+ hours
Difficulty: Moderate to challenging paddling
Nearest town: Flamingo
Season: Fall, winter, and early spring
Fees: None
Highlights: Everglades interior, the Gulf of Mexico
Hazards: Waves, strong tides

Getting there: Coming from Homestead or Florida City on Florida's east coast, the entrance to Everglades National Park is off CR 997 (Krome Avenue), which is off US 1. Go through the main gate onto FL 9336 and follow the main road down 38 miles and past a few ponds down to the boat ramp. From Flamingo you can either paddle or take a powerboat shuttle to the launch site. You can arrange for a shuttle at the marina in Flamingo. Northwest Cape is northwest from Flamingo; head west around the mainland and then north. It's approximately 20 miles from Flamingo.

The Paddle

This daylong trek is an outside route and could be part of a multiday paddle where, heading northwest, you would follow the mainland around to your right and pass several campgrounds (Clubhouse Beach, East Cape, and Middle Cape up to Northwest Cape) in approximately 18.0 miles.

For this paddle, launch from the beach area at Northwest Cape and head north. Paddle along the shore for a while, passing Little Sable Creek and then another creek that links up with Little Sable Creek. This creek takes you into and out of Lake Ingraham. Watch the mangroves here. The trees are highly compacted, vying for sunlight. Their twisted roots seem to prop one another up.

Continue paddling and reach the south end of Big Sable Creek. You have paddled 3.0 miles now. There is a fjord here that extends for almost 1.0 mile. From the bay of the inlet, you may be able to see the tip of Shark Island. Tall mangroves dot the shoreline up the northwest coastline past Big Sable Creek. Tidal creeks have serrated the shore, forming small coves. The bay between Shark River and the main coast narrows to the Little Shark River channel. Paddle up the bay (north). Pass an intricate light marker at the mouth of the Little Shark River and enter the river. (If you continue

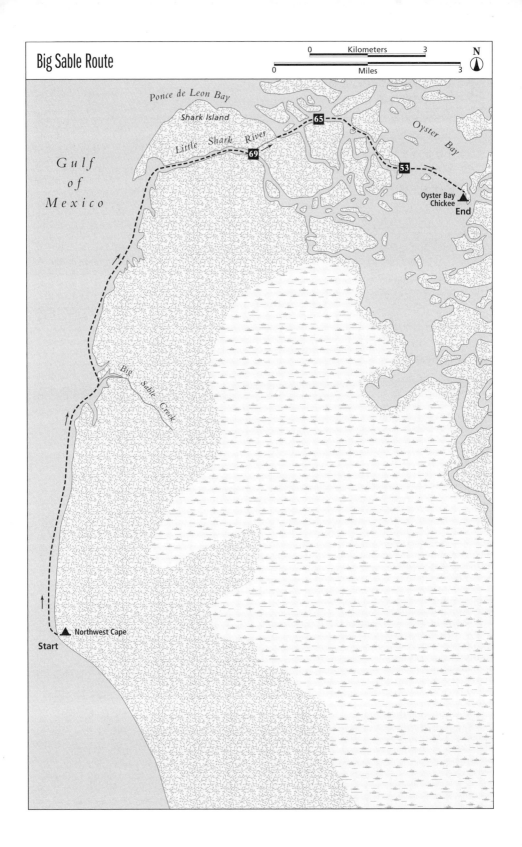

up the Gulf Coast, you will need to paddle 4.0 miles across Ponce De Leon Bay to the Graveyard Creek campsite.)

The route is marked up to Oyster Bay with red and green Coast Guard markers. Continue paddling and make a turn, heading east up the Little Shark River. You will encounter strong tides here due to the volume of water traversing. The river is very wide here, several hundred feet, and intersected by several smaller creeks. You will not see another marker until the Little Shark River splits into a channel to the northeast at Marker 69. Follow the now-narrow Little Shark River, watching for powerboats in the channel. Paddle this route for about 0.25 mile before meeting up with multiple other channels that are part of the Shark River network. This area drains most of the freshwater from the Everglades south to the Gulf. However, due to the confluence the water will be brackish, even salty.

Follow the markers until Marker 65, and then head southeast toward Oyster Bay. Continue paddling south to the west end of Oyster Bay (Marker 53). You have traveled 12.0 miles from the Northwest Cape. Turn and head east across the bay toward a cluster of islands. Oyster Bay Chickee is set back against the outlying islands. Paddle to the chickee in the lagoon, where your route ends at 13.0 miles.

Options: Continue to the Wilderness Waterway by following the markers for about 0.5 mile. Shark River Chickee is located 3.0 miles from Oyster Bay, through the Shark Cutoff. Heading south will take you to Joe River Chickee in 4.0 miles and to Watson River Chickee in 8.0 miles, through Cormorant Pass.

22 Nine Mile Pond Loop

The loop is not actually 9 miles, as the waterway is called. It was give its name because the pond was 9 miles from the original Park Service ranger station at Coot Bay Pond. The trail is marked with poles to help you navigate through the mangroves, other trees, and small islands. Water levels will vary depending on the season, and the prairies can be very dry. Check with the Park Service before venturing out. Also, there won't be any dry areas along this route where you can stop and stretch your legs. Canoe rentals are available here from the Park Service.

County: Miami-Dade
Start/End: Nine Mile Pond, off the main Everglades National Park road (FL 9336)
Distance: 5.2 miles round-trip
Approximate float time: Approximately 3 hours
Difficulty: Easy to moderate paddling on a marked trail

Nearest town: Flamingo
Season: Fall, winter, and early spring
Fees: Park entrance fee
Highlights: Birds, flora and fauna, alligators
Hazards: Confusing landscape
Getting there: Coming from Homestead or Florida City on Florida's east coast, the entrance to Everglades National Park is off

CR 997 (Krome Avenue), which is off US 1. Go through the main gate onto FL 9336 and follow the main road down about 25 miles. The entrance for Nine Mile Pond and the canoe trail is on your left. Go to the eastern part of the parking lot.

The Paddle

Put in at Nine Mile Pond, just off the main park road coming from Flamingo. Here you will find saw grass and the markers (poles) for the canal. This is also a great place to see alligators.

Enter a mangrove tunnel and emerge onto a small prairie. The water is relatively clear, and you can see small fish and minnows. Paddle through mangroves for a while, and then enter saw grass. As you paddle through the saw grass, around Marker 42, the prairie opens up more. Beyond this are palm tree islands.

After entering the prairie, follow the markers to the right into a mangrove tunnel and paddle along for the loop. (Option: To shorten the loop, instead of taking the right turn, continue straight, past Marker 44 to 44A, and across the prairie to Marker 82. Paddle left here and finish your loop.)

Canoe rentals are available from the park service, like these near Nine Mile Pond.

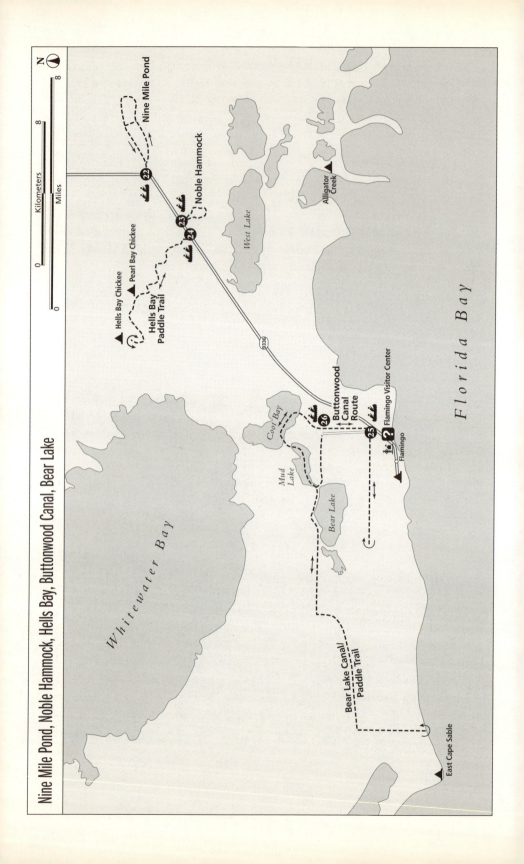

On the longer route described here, the prairie opens up to another, thicker saw grass waterway. Turn left at Marker 73, heading westward. The area is lined with hammocks and palms along the shore. Continue paddling past Marker 80, where you will enter an area with mangroves and palms. From here you will enter an alligator pond and bend to the left, paddling through the saw grass into yet another pond. Propel yourself through this pond into another. You should be able to see the parking area where you started. You have completed the loop.

23 Noble Hammock

This is a great short paddle for beginners or for the family. Noble Hammock is reported to have been a haven for moonshiners in the early twentieth century. This route, with its twists and turns and a maze of mangroves, is a great short trip for those with limited time. This is also a good area for fishing, so bring your gear. If it has been dry for a while, you may want to check water levels with the Park Service before heading out.

County: Monroe
Start/End: Noble Hammock, off the main Everglades National Park road (FL 9336)
Distance: 2.0 miles round-trip
Approximate float time: 1 to 2 hours
Difficulty: Easy paddling
Nearest town: Flamingo
Season: Fall, winter, and early spring
Fees: Park entrance fee
Highlights: Shady, tree hammock

Hazards: Confusing landscape; first route to dry out during the winter season
Getting there: Coming from Homestead or Florida City on Florida's east coast, the entrance to Everglades National Park is off CR 997 (Krome Avenue), which is off US 1. Go through the main gate onto FL 9336 and follow the main road down a little more than 25 miles. The entrance for Noble Hammock is on your left past Nine Mile Pond, approximately 1.5 miles.

The Paddle

Launch from the ramp off the main park road, CR 9336, if coming from Flamingo in the south of the park. Turn right on the creek and follow the markers. The small ponds and passageways are beautiful to take in. Just don't forget to watch the markers—it is easy to get lost in here. The water may be brackish due to the decomposition of native plants. Paddle through the narrow waterways, but be careful to avoid going off-trail into any small bay. The canal leads into tiny creeks, which are shaded by the mangroves. You may want to get out and stretch around Marker 45; however, there is little or no dry land to stand on.

Keep paddling through the overgrown waterway. Not far up on your right, a sign designates Noble Hammock. There's a small landing here where you can get out and explore. If you don't mind hacking through overgrown trails, you can find the

These are Black Mangroves, as you can tell from the "prop roots," the pneumataphores.

remains of Bill Noble's Prohibition-era moonshine brick furnace. The heavy growth helped obscure the still.

Back in your canoe or kayak, continue paddling to your right. This creek is a haven for anglers of any level. Fishermen can pull in bluegill, largemouth bass, gar, and tilapia.

You will soon come to a park road and a small dock, about 100 yards from where you started.

24 Hells Bay Paddle Trail

This route is usually overgrown and the put-in is a small area off the main road through the park. There are markers to help you find it, but little parking. Water depth goes from shallow to 5 feet deep. The bottom of this stream is limestone, and you will find wax myrtle and coco plum trees along the way. You can stop and stretch at Lard Can and then continue on to Pearl Bay Chickee before following another creek to Hells Bay Chickee.

County: Monroe
Start: Hells Bay ramp off the main Everglades National Park road (FL 9336)
End: Depends on how far you wish to paddle
Distance: 3.0 miles to Lard Can campsite; 3.5 miles to Pearl Bay Chickee; 5.5 miles to Hells Bay Chickee—all one-way
Approximate float time: 2 to 4 hours
Difficulty: Easy paddling; a little confusing
Nearest town: Flamingo
Season: Fall, winter, and early spring
Fees: Park entrance fee
Highlights: Birds, mangrove tunnels, marked trail, leads to East River

Hazards: Confusing landscape
Getting there: Coming from Homestead or Florida City on Florida's east coast, the entrance to Everglades National Park is off CR 997 (Krome Avenue), which is off US 1. Go through the main gate onto FL 9336 and follow the main road down about 25 miles. The entrance to Hells Bay is about 2 miles further down from Nine Mile Pond, on the right and just past Noble Hammock. Follow the signs off the main road. There is a little ramp, somewhat hidden by trees, and a shoulder opposite where you can park.

The Paddle

Hells Bay Paddle Trail twists and turns through small streams and ponds. This used to be an alligator trail. The bottom of the waterway is limestone, the base for much of

Hells Bay launch sites. As you can see, it's crowded with numerous trees and aptly named.

the Everglades. Nearby on land you will find wax myrtle and coco plum trees. The waterway can be shallow with vegetation and then up to 5 feet deep. Paddlers can stop and stretch around Marker 80. The creek meanders northwest, passing a patch of paurotis palm.

The stream enters a small to medium-size bay at Marker 154. If you look to the east between Markers 155 and 156 across a small bay, you should be able to see the campsite for Lard Can. The campsite should be marked by PVC poles on the shore. You are about 3.0 miles from the launch ramp. This is a great place to rest and enjoy the tropical hammock with its ferns, palms, and coco plums. The Calusa Indians used to camp on this area of hard ground.

Back on the water, continue paddling northwest, following the markers (increasing in numerical order). Follow the creek to Pearl Bay. The wheelchair-accessible chickee is on your left at the north end of the bay. At this point you are about 1.0 mile past Lard Can. Head southwest from here, entering another creek.

This creek is longer and comes out in a bay engulfed by mangroves. Look for another creek that will take you to Hells Bay. The waterway widens around Marker 177. You will see another chickee, Hells Bay, past a few small islands. It should take about an hour to arrive here from Pearl Bay.

25 Buttonwood Canal Route

This waterway partially connects Flamingo to Everglade City through the Wilderness Waterway. The route is also used by powerboats to get to Whitewater Bay and northward. Popular with tour boats and tourists, this is an easy paddle with lots of foliage to admire. After you paddle for a few short miles, you will need to portage a short distance to the canal that will take you to Bear Lake.

County: Monroe
Start/End: Gravel launch site before marina, on the main Everglades National Park road (FL 9336) in Flamingo
Distance: 5.0 miles one-way
Approximate float time: 3 hours
Difficulty: Easy paddling
Nearest town: Flamingo
Season: Fall, winter, and early spring
Fees: Park entrance fee
Highlights: Connects Whitewater Bay to Florida Bay

Hazards: Powerboats
Connectors: Snake Bight, East Cape, First National Bank Route, Joe River, East River
Getting there: Coming from Homestead or Florida City on Florida's east coast, the entrance to Everglades National Park is off CR 997 (Krome Avenue), which is off US 1. Go through the main gate onto FL 9336 and follow the main road all the way down, approximately 37 miles, to Flamingo. There's a gravel launch site just before the marina. Buttonwood Canal is just off to your right.

The Paddle

From the boat ramp at Flamingo, head north on the Buttonwood Canal. The Park Service built the canal in 1956–57 so that boaters could access Whitewater Bay without going into the Gulf. The shores are lined with mangroves, but you can also see mahogany, gumbo-limbo, Jamaica dogwood, Brazilian pepper, and buttonwood, as well as cactus. If you look to your left, you can see limestone, Florida's bedrock. Bear Lake Road runs parallel to the canal.

The canal runs south, as does the limestone and trees as you paddle into Bear Lake Canoe Trail. You have paddled 2.0 miles at this point and will need to portage your canoe or kayak. Use the dock and trail to take you to the canal that heads to Bear Lake and beyond.

Follow the Buttonwood Canal on a northeastern trail. This will take you into Coot Bay, where you may encounter wind working against you. The bay is marked and will take you into Tarpon Creek.

You will see manatee warning signs as you enter Tarpon Creek. This is labeled as a "no wake" zone; however, boaters don't always heed this. Flanked by mangroves, the wide creek heads into Whitewater Bay. At Marker 10 you will have paddled 5.0 miles from the dock.

Options: Hells Bay Chickee is 6.0 miles farther, on the East River. It is 12.0 miles to Coast Guard Marker 40, at Cormorant Pass. It is 6.0 miles to South Joe Chickee using the Joe River route.

26 Bear Lake Canal/Paddle Trail (in the Backcountry)

NOTE: Check the status of this route before heading out. It was impassable due to damage from Hurricanes Katrina and Wilma in 2005; however, as this guide went to press, the park service was clearing it.

This trail follows the old Homestead Canal, built in the 1920s to drain Cape Sable for future development. The canal has become overgrown in the ensuing years, and mangroves have returned to the area. Beware of the mosquitoes! A plug at the East Cape Canal prevents tides from flowing into the canal. Dependent on rainwater and inflow from the freshwater Glades between the canoe trail and Whitewater Bay, this trail can be too shallow to paddle and then too muddy to walk through. Portages are required on this route. The first is a 160-yard carry from Buttonwood Canal to the beginning of Bear Lake. The second, this one a little shorter, is between Homestead and East Cape Canal.

County: Monroe
Start: Buttonwood Canal, 2 miles north from Flamingo
End: Depends entirely on how far you wish to paddle
Distance: 2 miles one-way to Bear Lake; 11.5 miles one-way to Cape Sable
Approximate float time: 2 to 6 hours
Difficulty: Easy paddling; portage required
Nearest town: Flamingo
Season: Fall, winter, and early spring
Fees: Park entrance fee
Highlights: No motorboats, shaded by mangroves

Hazards: Overgrown area, mosquitoes; incoming tides from the Gulf can prevent paddlers from exiting the East Cape Canal.
Campsites: East Cape Sable
Getting there: Coming from Homestead or Florida City on Florida's east coast, the entrance to Everglades National Park is off CR 997 (Krome Avenue), which is off US 1. Go through the main gate onto FL 9336 and follow the main road all the way down, 37 miles to Flamingo. There's a gravel launch site just before the marina (same put-in as for Buttonwood Canal Route), about one mile north of the marina.

The Paddle

This historic waterway is narrow, with tropical plants and trees. It may be impassable between markers 13 and 17 during the dry season.

Launch from a wooden dock at Bear Lake Canoe Trail, 2 miles north from Flamingo and begin paddling west under a canopy of mangrove trees. This is the Homestead Canal and the route will be very shallow and muddy. This 2.0-mile-long tunnel, which will take you from the Buttonwood Canal to Bear Lake, can be overgrown with prop roots from mangroves. Footpaths used to parallel the canal to Bear Lake. You will see a turn that will take you into Mud Lake, heading north; however, you want to stay on a straight westerly course, taking you through Bear Lake. This lake should be open after you come through the long tunnel.

Continue paddling west, following the markers (PVC) until you reach Gator Lake. Next, jog left (south) and then right (west again), and pass through a shallow lake. Paddle past more small islands, and then reach the canal again, heading south. When you reach the dam at East Cape Canal, you have traveled about 9.5 miles. You will need to get out and carry your canoe/kayak over the dam—and hope for an outgoing tide. This canal is wider than the Bear Lake Canoe Trail and heads straight south toward Florida Bay and the Gulf of Mexico.

At the mouth of the bay, it is 1.0 mile west to East Cape Sable campsite.

27 Mud Lake Loop

Enjoy a moderate loop through various lakes in a quiet, secluded area. This route can be tricky, with some shallow areas and downed trees and requires some portaging. The route can be very narrow. As you paddle into Mud Lake, you will find plenty of birds. The route starts north through a small man-made tunnel to Coot Bay and on to Buttonwood Canal.

County: Monroe
Start/End: Off gravel road just before the marina, on the main Everglades National Park road (FL 9336) in Flamingo
Distance: 6.8-mile loop from Coot Bay Pond
Approximate float time: 3 to 4 hours
Difficulty: Easy paddling; some portage required
Nearest town: Flamingo
Season: Fall, winter, and early spring
Fees: Park entrance fee
Highlights: Quiet, old canal route, marked trail; motorboats prohibited on Mud Lake, Bear Lake and the Bear Lake Canal
Hazards: Shallow; occasionally impassable
Getting there: Coming from Homestead or Florida City on Florida's east coast, the entrance to Everglades National Park is off CR 997 (Krome Avenue), which is off US 1. Go through the main gate onto FL 9336 and follow the main road all the way down, approximately 37 miles to Flamingo. Just before the marina you will see a dirt/gravel road off to your right (if you are heading down). This is the launch site.

The Paddle

You'll enjoy a variety of habitats on this loop, which connects the Buttonwood Canal, Coot Bay, Mud Lake, and the Bear Lake Canoe Trail.

Beginning your trek from Coot Bay Pond, paddle north into a mangrove tunnel and into Coot Bay. This area is very quiet; it is also very narrow and may have downed trees. Coot Bay also connects to the Wilderness Waterway. This loop connects to the Buttonwood Canal on your left (south) and then follows a small creek to Mud Lake. Birding is usually good in Mud Lake.

You can continue paddling through Mud Lake on to Bear Lake Canoe Trail and follow the old drainage canal to the newer Buttonwood Canal. However, in order to get to Buttonwood, you will need to portage 160-plus yards through thick vegetation and mosquitoes. This route loops back around to Coot Bay Pond via the Buttonwood Canal and Coot Bay.

Paddle north around one of the landings in Coot Bay Pond to a small opening to a tunnel. This small man-made tunnel, wide enough for a canoe and bordered by occasional palm trees, will take you into Coot Bay. Paddle west into Coot Bay, toward Marker 3 and the Buttonwood Canal. Continue paddling north, following the markers, and pass a shortcut to Whitewater Bay. Continue along the south shore of Coot Bay to a PVC pipe marker at 2.0 miles signaling a creek that leads to Mud Lake.

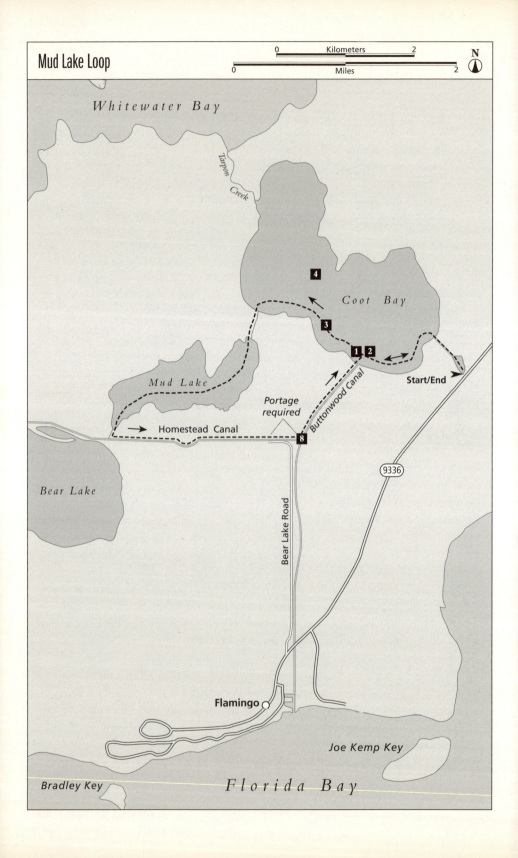

This shady, narrow waterway is made even narrower by dozens of fallen trees. Mangroves line the area, offering shade and habitat for birds and other animals. Emerge onto Mud Lake, where you will find markers and small islands. As you paddle south and west across this appealing lake, take note of the water and trees in the area.

Head toward the southwest corner of the lake and look for a creek that connects to Bear Lake Canoe Trail. Depending on the time of year, this area can be overgrown. Turn left here, heading east.

The Bear Lake Canoe Trail follows the old Homestead Canal. This canal was built in the 1920s alongside a road meant to connect Florida City to Cape Sable. The canal is filling in with mangrove roots and vegetation, making paddling shallow and difficult. Insects can be a real nuisance on the 2.0-mile trek to the portage. When you reach the trail, carry your canoe or kayak to your left toward two wooden poles. At the landing of Buttonwood Canal, you will put in and paddle northeast on the waterway. It will be wider here.

Come to Coot Bay; you're 6.0 miles from your launch site at this point. Paddle east toward another marker and follow this small creek to Coot Bay Pond. Continue paddling through the mangrove tunnel to complete the loop, finishing your paddle at 6.8 miles.

You'll enjoy a variety of habitats on this loop that connects the Buttonwood Canal, Coot Bay, Mud Lake, and the Bear Lake Canoe Trail. These are accessible from the Bear Lake trailhead or Coot Bay Pond. Motors are prohibited on Mud Lake, Bear Lake, and the Bear Lake Canal. These routes are not always passable during parts of the year.

28 Whitewater Bay Route

Whitewater Bay is a large area of water where powerboats and their wake can be a hindrance, even for experienced paddlers. However, the markers will aid in navigation for both experienced and novice paddlers. Starting in Tarpon Creek, you will paddle through Whitewater Bay, north and west, and into the Roberts River, passing a few islands before coming to the Watson River Chickee. Once past Midway Keys, you will be on the Wilderness Waterway.

County: Monroe
Start: Marker 10, Whitewater Bay (launch from Coot Bay)
End: Marker 40 in Cormorant Pass
Distance: 12.0 miles one-way to Marker 40 in Cormorant Pass (add approximately 3 miles from Coot Bay Pond to Marker 10)

Approximate float time: All day
Difficulty: Moderate paddling
Nearest town: Flamingo
Season: Fall, winter, and early spring
Fees: Park entrance fee
Highlights: Includes part of Wilderness Waterway, marked route, multiple connecting rivers

Hazards: Wind, powerboats, waves

Getting there: Coming from Homestead or Florida City on Florida's east coast, the entrance to Everglades National Park is off CR 997, Krome Avenue, which is off US 1. Go through the main gate onto FL 9336 and follow the main road down, approximately 30 miles to Coot Bay, located on your right after West Lake Canoe Trail.

The Paddle

Launch from Coot Bay Pond, off the main road (FL 9336). Paddle north and west towards Coot Bay, and then paddle through Coot Bay looking for the Tarpon Creek pass. Through this small lake you will see a few markers along the way (3, 4, and 8), which will lead you into Tarpon Creek.

On this trek you will leave from the southeastern most point of Whitewater Bay, near Tarpon Creek. This is west of Coot Bay and Mud Lake.

As you come out of Tarpon Creek near Marker 10, the water will be about 4 feet deep. It will get a little deeper through the open bay. Look north and slightly west for your markers. Watching boat traffic can be a benefit—you can follow their lead. However, if you stay to the right of their path, you will be able to paddle with less interference.

Paddle between a few islands and continue heading north and west to Marker 18. You have traveled 3.0 miles since Marker 10 at Tarpon Creek. You will be in open water through Whitewater bay unless you go into a river.

From here Roberts River is northeast. Continue paddling through the bay, through the Midway Keys, just after Marker 23. You will paddle between these larger islands on a narrow and shallower pass. This entire bay is part of the Wilderness Waterway, which runs 99 miles between Flamingo and Everglades City. Continue paddling into the open waters again to Marker 30—a total of 6.5 miles from Tarpon Creek.

Paddling another 3.0 miles northeast from Marker 34 will take you to Watson River Chickee (Marker 34 is 8.0 miles from Tarpon Creek). As you paddle through the bay, you will pass several islands, with mangroves farther ahead on both sides.

Pass between the two smaller mangrove islands and continue heading northwest toward a shoreline ahead. There are numerous islands consisting of mangrove trees here. Look for Marker 40, which will take you into Cormorant Pass if you continue going north and west. This is the end of Whitewater Bay route.

Option: Taking a sharp right at Marker 40 will take you back along the mangrove-lined shores to Watson River and other rivers to the east. The Watson River Chickee is 3.0 miles from this point (east and south).

Cormorant Pass is marked and slices through the islands. The current can be strong in this area. Oyster Bay Chickee is 1.0 mile into the pass. From here you can access a variety of rivers and the Wilderness Waterway.

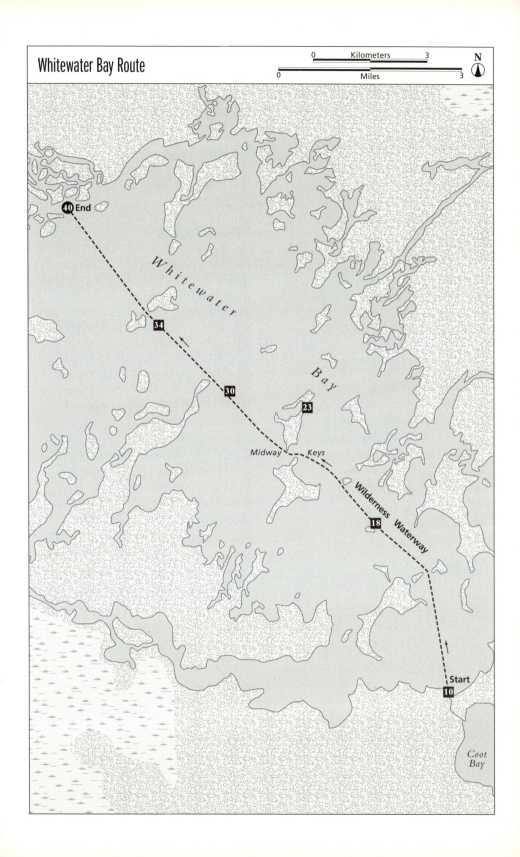

29 Labyrinth Route

This route is challenging as well as rewarding. You will be paddling a labyrinth of streams from the Shark River into Whitewater Bay—with no markers to aid you along the way. This long, tedious paddle will exercise your nerves and your chart-reading dexterity. While paddling you will need to keep one eye on your navigational chart and another on your position.

County: Monroe
Start: Shark River Chickee
End: Watson River Chickee
Distance: 6.0 miles one-way; paddling from Flamingo, add approximately 23+ more miles
Approximate float time: 3 to 4 hours; or more than one day
Difficulty: Mild to moderate paddling; challenging navigation—bring your compass and charts
Nearest town: Flamingo
Season: Fall, winter, and early spring
Fees: Park entrance fee; fee for shuttle to site unless paddling from other areas
Highlights: No powerboats, quiet
Hazards: Challenging navigation, getting lost
Campsites: Shark River and Watson River Chickees
Connectors: Cutoff Route, Cormorant Pass, Graveyard Creek

Getting there: Coming from Homestead or Florida City on Florida's east coast, the entrance to Everglades National Park is off CR 997 (Krome Avenue), which is off US 1. Go through the main gate onto FL 9336 and follow the main road all the way down, 38 miles to Flamingo. There is a marina, store, facilities, and ramp. You can also arrange for a shuttle to meet you here. To get to Shark River Chickee from Flamingo, you would need to paddle west and north around the mainland, following the coastline past East Cape, Middle Cape, and Northwest Cape campsites (20 miles), continuing north to Little Shark River and then turning in, heading east. Continue paddling east and slightly south, looking for Markers, 69, 68, and down until almost 64. When you see Marker 64, you will want to head around the northeast tip of this island to stay on your heading on Little Shark River. This will take you to Shark River Chickee.

The Paddle

This internal route can be part of a multiday adventure or a powerboat shuttle. You could shuttle from Flamingo or Coot Bay up to Watson River Chickee and head northwest. Or, from the outside, you could shuttle from Flamingo and around the coast up to Ponce De Leon Bay and then paddle up to Shark River Chickee.

Check the tidal flow at the Shark River Chickee and on your chart before venturing out. If the tide is just turning as you are heading out, then it will remain the same during your paddle.

As you head out, the river meanders south and west for a while, with a few twists and turns through the mangroves. Paddle about 1.5 miles or so before coming to a split in the river, and then the maze begins.

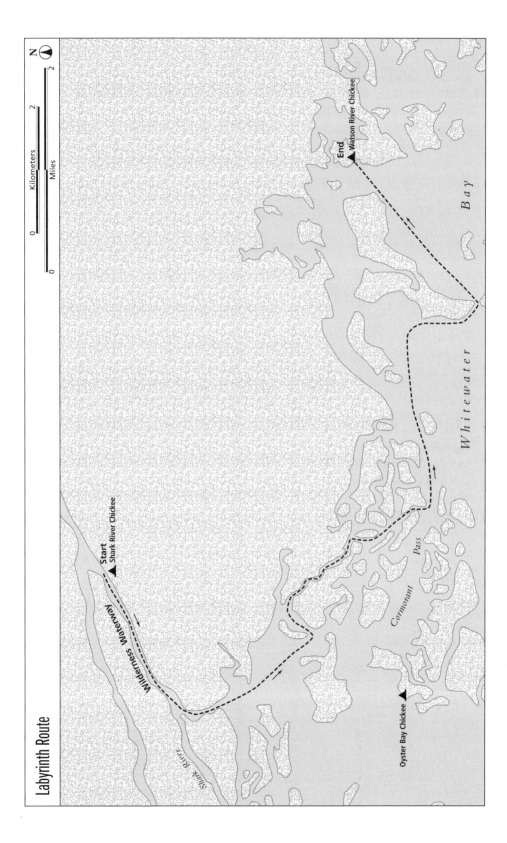

There is more than one way through the maze. It is imperative that you take your time and know where you are as you are paddling around these meandering streams. There is no one specific route to guide you here—you are more or less on your own. Keep your chart out (and dry), and map your way as you paddle (slowly) through the tangled web of trees and streams. Looking back every so often may help you if you need to backtrack.

When you finally reach Whitewater Bay, you can breath a sigh of relief. You did it! Paddle southeast and past a few large islands on your right. The Watson River Chickee will appear ahead, on a mangrove island facing north.

Option: From Watson River Chickee to Roberts River Chickee is 6.0 miles using the Cutoff Route.

30 Cormorant Pass

This is an internal route in Whitewater Bay. After launching from Joe River Chickee, you will go north through Oyster Bay. There are multiple connector routes along the way that can take you to many islands in Whitewater Bay and along the Wilderness Waterway. Watch the markers for points of reference. If the numbers are increasing, you are heading north; if they are decreasing, you are heading south.

County: Monroe
Start: Cove of Joe River Chickee
End: Watson River Chickee
Distance: 12.0 miles one-way
Approximate float time: All day
Difficulty: Mild to moderate paddling, depending on tide, wind, and powerboat traffic
Nearest town: Flamingo
Season: Fall, winter, and spring
Fees: Park entrance fee
Highlights: Mangrove islands
Hazards: Motorboats
Connector routes: Labyrinth, Joe River, Big Sable, Whitewater Bay, Cutoff Route
Campsites: Joe River, Oyster Bay, Watson River Chickees
Getting there: Coming from Homestead or Florida City on Florida's east coast, the entrance to Everglades National Park is off CR 997 (Krome Avenue), which is off US 1. Go through the main gate onto FL 9336 and follow the main road all the way down, 38 miles to Flamingo. There is a marina, store, facilities, and ramp. You can also arrange for a shuttle here. To get to Joe River Chickee from Flamingo, you would need to paddle west and north around the mainland, following the coastline past East Cape, Middle Cape, and Northwest Cape campsites (20 miles), continuing north to Little Shark River and then turning in, heading east. Continue paddling east and slightly south, looking for Markers 69, 68, and down until almost 64. When you see Marker 64, turn and head south between the larger islands and then into the open water in Oyster Bay. Joe River Chickee will be up ahead in a group of islands in a cove.

110 Paddling Everglades National Park

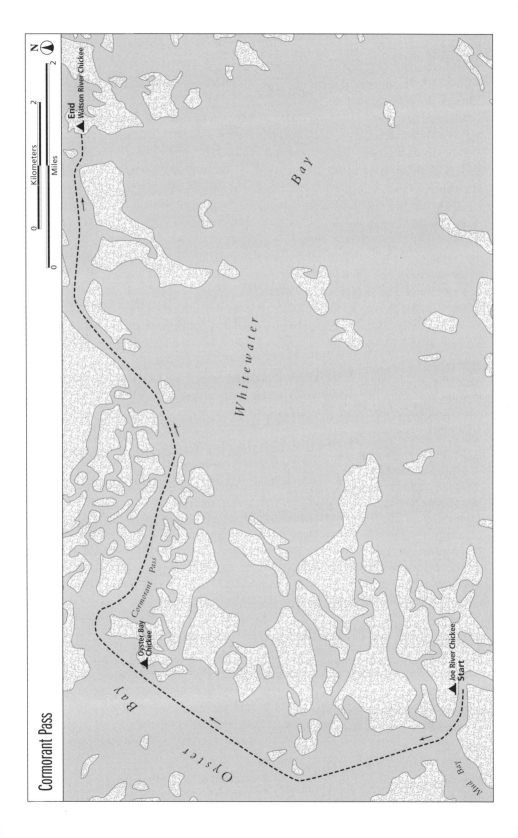

The Paddle

This is an internal route, part of a multiday paddle trip or possible powerboat shuttle through Whitewater Bay.

Launch from the cove of Joe River Chickee, paddling north to the river past the PLEASE WATCH FOR MANATEES sign. Mud Bay will be on the left. Paddle into the open Oyster Bay, still heading north. You'll see small islands on the east.

Two miles out, Oyster Bay widens and the islands begin to disappear. Straight ahead in the bay is a solitary island. Oyster Bay Chickee is housed in a cluster of islands.

Continue paddling toward the shoreline of mangrove trees. The islands become more apparent as you paddle inland. The chickee, 4.0 miles from your start point, is on your right. The waterway through Cormorant Pass and into Oyster Bay is 4 to 5 feet deep.

To reach the Gulf from Shark River Island, it's 6.0 miles from Oyster Bay Chickee through the Big Sable route and 3.0 miles through the Shark Cutoff Route to Shark River Chickee. If you run into channel markers, you have gone too far.

As you leave Oyster Bay Chickee, paddle north past Shark River Chickee. Head for the markers north of the chickee, looking for Marker 50. From here head southeast and follow the markers through Cormorant Pass and around several small islands. If the channel numbers are increasing, you are going north on the Wilderness Waterway. The marker numbers should be decreasing. Continue paddling south to Marker 40. From here it is 12.0 miles to Tarpon Creek, at the south end of Whitewater Bay.

Leave Cormorant Pass and the Wilderness Waterway and head northeast along Whitewater Bay, paddling between mangrove islands. Paddle along the open waterway to Watson River Chickee. Watson River Chickee is located around the bend of the larger mangrove islands. It is on the south end of one of the larger islands and faces north. You have paddled 12.0 miles.

Options: From here it is approximately 6.0 miles southeast to Roberts River Chickee via the Cutoff Route and 6.0 miles northwest to Shark River Chickee on the Labyrinth Route.

31 Lane River Route

This route starts out from Hells Bay, which may be a little overgrown depending on when you go, and heads north into a channel. The route continues past several islands to Lane Bay, Lane Bay Chickee, and a rookery. When the river narrows, just follow the mangroves around. The route ends at Lane and Robert Rivers.

County: Monroe
Start: Hells Bay Chickee
End: Lane and Roberts Rivers
Distance: 5.0 miles one-way; add 5.5 miles if launching from Hells Bay (more than 20 miles round-trip)
Approximate float time: 2 to 3 hours; add 2.5 hours when launching from Hells Bay each way
Difficulty: Mild paddling
Nearest town: Flamingo
Season: Fall, winter, and early spring
Fees: Park entrance fee
Highlights: Birding
Hazards: Tricky navigation
Campsites: Hells Bay and Lane Bay Chickees
Getting there: For this internal route, you will need to launch from FL 9336, the main road through Everglades National Park. Coming from Homestead or Florida City on Florida's east coast, the entrance to Everglades National Park is off CR 997 (Krome Avenue), which is off US 1. Go through the main gate onto FL 9336 and follow this road down about 27 miles. The entrance for Hells Bay will be marked; it's off a gravel road on the right. This is the put-in for Hells Bay and you will need to paddle it (adding miles and time to your route) in order to reach Hells Bay Chickee. Hells Bay Paddle Trail twists and turns through small streams and ponds. The waterway can be shallow with vegetation and then up to 5 feet deep. Paddlers can stop and stretch around Marker 80. The creek meanders northwest, passing a patch of paurotis palm.

The stream enters a small to medium-size bay at Marker 154. If you look to the east between Markers 155 and 156 across a small bay, you should be able to see the campsite for Lard Can. The campsite should be marked by PVC poles on the shore. You are about 3.0 miles from the launch ramp.

Continue paddling northwest, following the markers (increasing in numerical order). Follow the creek to Pearl Bay.

The wheelchair-accessible chickee is on your left at the north end of the bay. At this point you are about 1.0 mile past Lard Can. Head southwest from here, entering another creek. This creek is longer and comes out in a bay engulfed by mangroves. Look for another creek that will take you to Hells Bay. The waterway widens around Marker 177. You will see another chickee, Hells Bay, past a few small islands. It should take about an hour to arrive here from Pearl Bay.

Follow the canoe trail past Lard Can Chickee and Pearl Bay. Hells Bay Chickee will be up ahead on your left.

The Paddle

A warped river linking Hells Bay and Roberts River, this is a complex area of small ponds, bays, and rivers—a good alternative to paddling in Whitewater Bay. The East River will connect you to Hells Bay.

Launch from Hells Bay Chickee and head north. Pay attention to the area—there may be more islands here than there are on your navigational chart. Don't head toward the large body of water (Whitewater Bay). Instead steer toward the 40-plus-foot-wide channel, which connects to a bay with copious petite islands. Continue paddling northwest through the bay into The Funnel—a wider creek that funnels you into Lane Bay.

As you paddle through Lane Bay, look around the islands for West Indies mahogany. You can identify this tree from its hard, brown fruit about the size of a pear. Lane Bay Chickee is ahead on the north side of the bay, sequestered in a tall hammock. You have traveled 2.5 miles from Hells Bay Chickee.

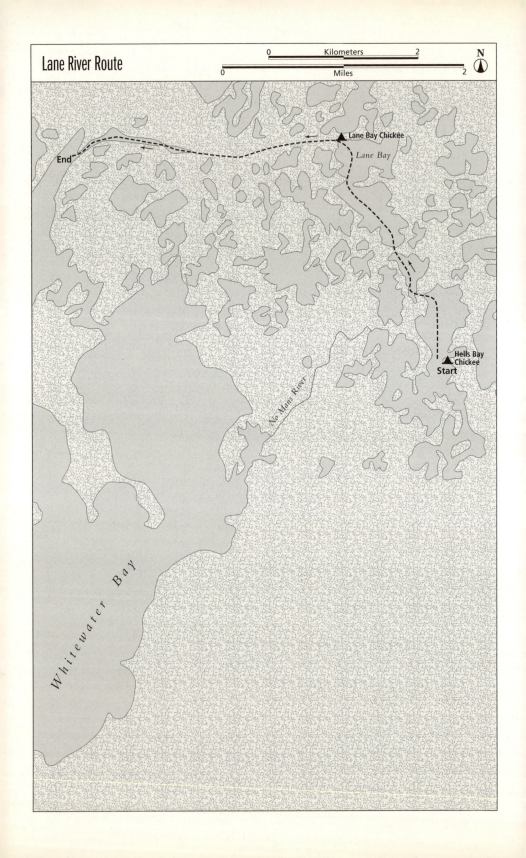

After leaving the chickee, you need to pay attention to your charts and navigation. It can be a little thorny. Keep to the western side of Lane River with mangroves and emaciated trees poking through. Look around here for both migrating and permanent avian residents, which can be plentiful in this ideal roosting area. The river runs about 50 to 80 feet across at this point, with a mud bottom that runs pretty deep.

The river narrows as you come to an island, about 1.0 mile from Lane Bay Chickee. As you paddle farther down the river, a creek merges with the river and it broadens. Follow the mangroves along the shore as they extend higher. Before the rivers merge, Lane River bends southwest, affording grand vistas. The creek narrows and ends where you find a warning sign about manatees. Lane River merges with Roberts River and widens into a bay. Paddle through the middle in a southbound course.

Options: From where the rivers merge, it's 2.5 miles to the Wilderness Waterway and Whitewater Bay. Also from the convergence, it is 2.5 miles up the Roberts River to the Roberts River Chickee.

32 North River Route

This route takes you from Whitewater Bay up the North River and past a few islands. The river meanders and gets narrower and then wider. On this quiet paddle you can take in the scenery of saw grass, feeder streams—even manatees.

County: Monroe
Start: Coast Guard Marker 30 in Whitewater Bay
End: Cutoff at North River
Distance: 4.5 miles one-way add approximatley 9.5 miles from Coot Bay Pond launch
Approximate float time: 2 hours; 4-plus hours round-trip, or multi-day paddle
Difficulty: Moderate paddling
Nearest town: Flamingo
Season: Fall and winter, possibly early spring
Fees: Park entrance fee; possible powerboat shuttle
Highlights: Quiet, manatees in the bay
Hazards: Wind, waves in Whitewater Bay
Connectors: The Cutoff Route
Getting there: This is an internal route. You can either paddle up to this channel marker (possible multiday trip), or get a powerboat lift through Whitewater Bay.

Launch from Coot Bay Pond, off the main road (FL 9336). Paddle north and west towards Coot Bay. Paddle through Coot Bay looking for the Tarpon Creek pass. Through this small lake you will see a few markers along the way; 3, 4 Markers and then 8 will lead you into Tarpon Creek.

As you come out of Tarpon Creek near Marker 10, the water will be about 4 feet deep. It will get a little deeper through the open bay. Look north and slightly west for your markers. Watching boat traffic can be a benefit—you can follow their lead. Stay to the right of their path and you will be able to paddle with less interference.

Paddle between a few islands and continue heading north and west to Marker 18. You have traveled 3.0 miles since Marker 10. You will be in open water through this bay, Whitewater.

From here Roberts River is northeast. Continue paddling through the bay and the

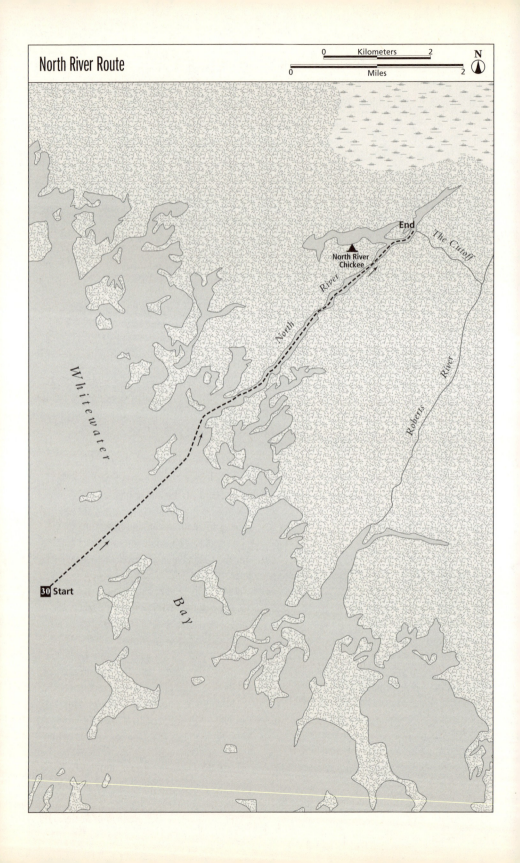

Midway Keys just after Marker 23. You will paddle between these larger islands on a narrow and shallower pass. This entire bay is part of the Wilderness Waterway, which runs 99 miles between Flamingo and Everglades City. Continue paddling into the open waters again to Marker 30—a total of 6.5 miles from Tarpon Creek.

The Paddle

Launching from Whitewater Bay, head northeast from Coast Guard Marker 30. Paddle by a few small islands on your right and left. Continue paddling toward the mainland until you reach a wide channel. This is the beginning of North River; the waterway will narrow considerably from here. Mangroves appear to block the waterway, but this is actually an island that forks the North River. You should see a warning sign for manatees in front of the island. At this point you have paddled about 3.0 miles.

Paddle either way around the island. Shortly after passing this island you will come to another island that splits the river. Continue around this one as well. As you head up the North River from here, the waterway is clear and deep. Water depth averages 5 feet through this channel, which is straight for the most part, with only minor turns.

The river alternately widens and narrow as you paddle northeast for almost 2.0 miles. In about 1.75 miles you will come to an intersection with the Cutoff Route. The Cutoff proper is ahead about 0.25 mile on your right (east). On the west side, an unnamed river leads to the North River Chickee. North River continues for 0.75 mile before splitting into smaller branches and then blending into the saw grass and a freshwater network of feeder streams.

Options: Turn around and head back the way you came in for a 9.0-mile round-trip (approximately 5 hours); or take the Cutoff Route east and then paddle down the Roberts River, making a big loop.

Another option is to turn left, opposite the Cutoff Route, and head south and west toward the North River Chickee. Paddle through a few lakes, taking a jog to the left (south) at about 90 degrees, and follow the waterway. After this second smaller pond, take another jog to the left, heading more southerly. Continue to follow this waterway back southwest into Whitewater Bay. You will pass North River Chickee on your left. The creek meanders about, trickling southwest along mangroves for a few miles before merging again with Whitewater Bay.

If you turn right and head into the Cutoff Route, it is mostly marsh with saw grass. Through the canal from North River to Roberts River, the route is about 1.5 miles. You may see a few feeder streams off to the sides before getting to the main river. Slowly you will start to turn to the right to head south. At this confluence turn right and south into the main part of Roberts River.

33 The Cutoff Route

You will experience a few different Everglades environments on this paddle. The route is located most directly between the Roberts and North Rivers but also connects to an unnamed river, thus connecting three campsites. These are all located northeast of Whitewater Bay in an area is referred to as "the backcountry." Once you are out in the keys, there are several routes you can take to Watson River Chickee.

County: Monroe
Start: Roberts River Chickee
End: Watson River Chickee
Distance: 6.0 miles one-way
Approximate float time: 3 hours
Difficulty: Mild paddling; moderate on Whitewater Bay
Nearest town: Flamingo
Season: Fall, winter, and early spring
Fees: Park entrance fee
Highlights: Quiet, good campsites
Hazards: Waves on Whitewater Bay
Campsites: Roberts River and Watson River Chickees
Connectors: Roberts River, North River, the Labyrinth, Cormorant Pass
Getting there: This is an internal route in Whitewater Bay. Enter Everglades National Park from Homestead and follow the main park road (FL 9336) approximately 30 miles down to Coot Bay. Launch from Coot Bay and paddle to the Roberts River Chickee (as part of a multiday trip), or arrange for a powerboat shuttle to the start point. To get to Roberts River Chickee by paddling, start out from Coot Bay Pond. Paddle north and west toward Coot Bay. Paddle through Coot Bay looking for the Tarpon Creek pass. Through this small lake you will see a few markers along the way; Markers 3, 4, and then 8 will lead you into the creek, Tarpon Creek.

As you come out of Tarpon Creek near Marker 10, the water will be about 4 feet deep. It will get a little deeper through the open bay. Look north and slightly west for your markers. Watching boat traffic can be a benefit—you can follow their lead. Stay to the right of their path and you will be able to paddle with less interference.

Paddle between a few islands and continue heading north and west to Marker 18. You have traveled 3.0 miles since Marker 10. You will be in open water through this bay, Whitewater. Launching from Marker 18, head northeast for a strait between a series of islands (keys) that forms a channel and leads to Roberts River. Continue paddling up the channel (northeast) as the river narrows. Turn to the right; the channel stays narrow for about 1.0 mile. It constricts even more after you pass the Lane River, marked with a warning sign for manatees. You have traveled about 2.5 miles.

Heading east on the Lane River will take you to the Hells Bay Chickee in about 5.0 miles. However, this route may be tricky to navigate—you have to go through lakes and small creeks heading east and then south.

Keep paddling up the Roberts River. The channel should still be deep and relatively narrow. Not far ahead is a merging of two creeks. Stay to the left, heading north. The river is fairly wide, about 50 feet across, for about 1.0 mile and then widens even more, now into a bay. This bay contains peninsulas and small creeks, which amble into the mangroves. Here, at the mouth of the bay, Roberts River Chickee is on your right. Behind the chickee is a tall hammock, set back off the river a little and protected.

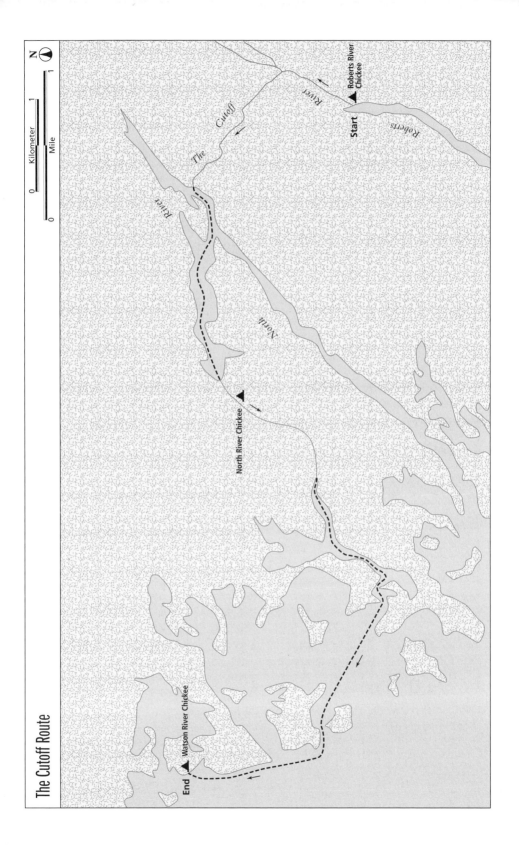

The Paddle

This route starts at Roberts River Chickee (you can reverse this based on where you may be coming from). Turn right and head north on the river, paddling past mangroves along the banks. The river narrows as you approach the Cutoff, which is ahead on your left. The mangroves may be down or overgrown above this connector. Another connector just north of this point links Lostman's and Rodgers Rivers. You may see remnants of an old shell mound along the river on the right before taking the Cutoff.

Take the left (northwest) stream and paddle among the solitude. Mangroves line the shores, but if you look beyond them you can see a saw grass prairie on the right. The Cutoff widens as you paddle down this stretch for about 1.0 mile before intersecting the North River. Ignore the North River (which heads south) and instead paddle west on another, wider, waterway.

This channel has a few minor twists and turns as it meanders southwest. You will go through some wider parts before the channel narrows into a southward-bound stream. Mangroves drape over the waterway along the shore. As you paddle south toward Whitewater Bay, you will see the North River Chickee—which really isn't on the North River but on a larger funnel stream west of the river—on a mangrove island to your left.

Whether you're just resting for a while or camping for the night, this chickee is quiet and secluded. After the chickee, continue heading south-southwest down the channel. Paddle along this deep channel until you come to a small island. Once around this island, the channel widen as you begin to enter Whitewater Bay. A mangrove key acts as a buffer between the river and the expansive Whitewater Bay.

Once in these keys, there are several routes you can take to head west toward the Watson River Chickee. Depending on the wind, and your experience, you can head farther out around the mangrove islands and ride the waves. If you opt for the outside loop—being carried by the waves for a little more action than gentle paddling—the water gets a little deeper.

Or you can paddle the channels on the northeast side between several of the islands. This will be a little crisscross amid the weather-beaten mangroves. The water in here is fairly shallow, 2 to 3 feet.

Look for the white manatee-warning sign in Whitewater Bay, which will direct you toward Watson River. The sign is north of the chickee, which is on a mangrove island facing the bay. Watson River Chickee offers a nice view of the bay, the mangroves, and the setting sun.

34 Roberts River Route

Launching in Whitewater Bay, you will have to navigate around several islands, using your chart to find the channel for Roberts River. This waterway meanders about and becomes very narrow for a while. The route passes Lane River and Hells Bay Chickee, eventually entering mangroves and reaching a tall hammock.

County: Monroe
Start: Marker 18 in Whitewater Bay
End: Roberts River Chickee
Distance: 5.5 miles one-way
Approximate float time: 3 to 4 hours
Difficulty: Mild paddling
Nearest town: Flamingo
Season: Fall, winter, and spring
Fees: Park entrance fee
Highlights: Quiet
Hazards: Wind
Campsites: Roberts River Chickee
Connectors: North River via Cutoff Route, Lane River to chickee and into Hells Bay
Getting there: This is an internal route in Whitewater Bay. Enter Everglades National Park from Homestead and follow the main park road (FL 9336), approximately 30 miles to Coot Bay Pond. Launch from Coot Bay Pond and paddle to Marker 18 (as part of a multiday trip), or arrange for a powerboat shuttle to the start point. Paddle north and west toward Coot Bay. Paddle through Coot Bay looking for the Tarpon Creek pass. Through this small lake you will see a few markers along the way; Markers 3, 4 and then 8 will lead you into Tarpon Creek.

As you come out of Tarpon Creek near Marker 10, the water will be about 4 feet deep. It will get a little deeper through the open bay. Look north and slightly west for your markers. Watching boat traffic can be a benefit—you can follow their lead. Stay to the right of their path and you will be able to paddle with less interference.

Paddle between a few islands and continue heading north and west to Marker 18. You have traveled 3.0 miles since Marker 10. You will be in open water through this bay, Whitewater.

The Paddle

Launching from Marker 18, head northeast for a strait between a series of islands (keys) that forms a channel and leads to Roberts River. Continue paddling up the channel (northeast) as the river narrows. Turn to the right; the channel stays narrow for about 1.0 mile. It constricts even more after you pass the Lane River, marked with a warning sign for manatees. You have traveled about 2.5 miles.

Heading east on the Lane River will take you to the Hells Bay Chickee in about 5.0 miles. However, this route may be tricky to navigate—you have to go through lakes and small creeks heading east and then south.

Keep paddling up the Roberts River. The channel should still be deep and relatively narrow. Not far ahead is a merging of two creeks. Stay to the left, heading north. The river is fairly wide, about 50 feet across, for about 1.0 mile and then widens even more, now into a bay. This bay contains peninsulas and small creeks, which amble into the mangroves. Here, at the mouth of the bay, Roberts River Chickee is on your

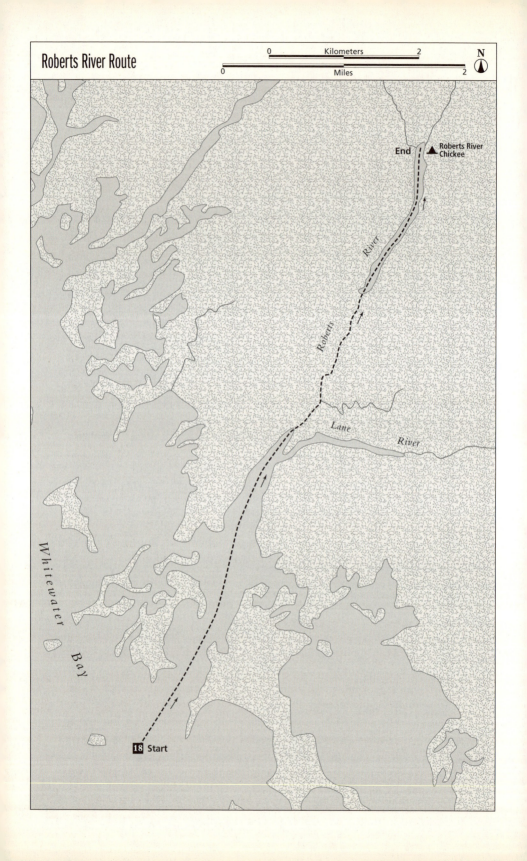

right. Behind the chickee is a tall hammock, set back off the river a little and protected. Here you will find some dry ground along with plants and ferns.

Options: From here you are 1.5 miles from North River and 3.0 miles from the North River Chickee.

35 East River Route

Getting on the right channel can be tricky if you're coming from Hells Bay and going to Whitewater. Other factors to keep in mind on this paddle are wind and tide. By staying near the shoreline, you can minimize both and you can enjoy the wildlife. The manatee warning sign is your signal you are nearing the East River. As you paddle up the river, you will see smaller creeks funneling off into bays.

County: Monroe
Start: Marker 10, Whitewater Bay; or from Coot Bay Pond through Coot Bay and Tarpon Creek
End: Hells Bay Chickee
Distance: 5.5 miles one-way (from Marker 10)
Approximate float time: 3 hours
Difficulty: Mild to moderate paddling
Nearest town: Flamingo
Season: Fall, winter, and early spring
Fees: Park entrance fee
Highlights: Bay, mangroves, manatees
Hazards: Powerboats, waves (bay side)
Getting there: To launch from Coot Bay (adding a few extra miles and time), enter Everglades National Park from Homestead and follow the main park road (FL 9336) approximately 30 miles to Coot Bay Pond. Paddle north and west towards Coot Bay. Paddle through Coot Bay looking for the Tarpon Creek pass. Through this small lake you will see a few markers along the way; Markers 3, 4, and then 8 will lead you into Tarpon Creek.

As you come out of Tarpon Creek near Marker 10, the water will be about 4 feet deep. It will get a little deeper through the open bay. Look north and slightly west for your markers. Watching boat traffic can be a benefit—you can follow their lead. Stay to the right of their path and you will be able to paddle with less interference.

The Paddle

This internal route in Whitewater Bay could be an all-day trip or part of a multiday adventure.

Starting from Marker 10 in the south end of Whitewater Bay, paddle northeast along the shoreline. Since you are in the open bay, there may be wind and waves. If you stay near the shoreline, you will not only be safer but will not get turned around and will see more wildlife.

When you've paddled about 3.0 miles, your path needs to go southeast, between Whitewater Bay and an island running north–south that safeguards the headwaters of the No Mans and East Rivers. Watch for a manatee sign; this marks the entrance to the East River. Paddle up the East River following the mangrove trees as they

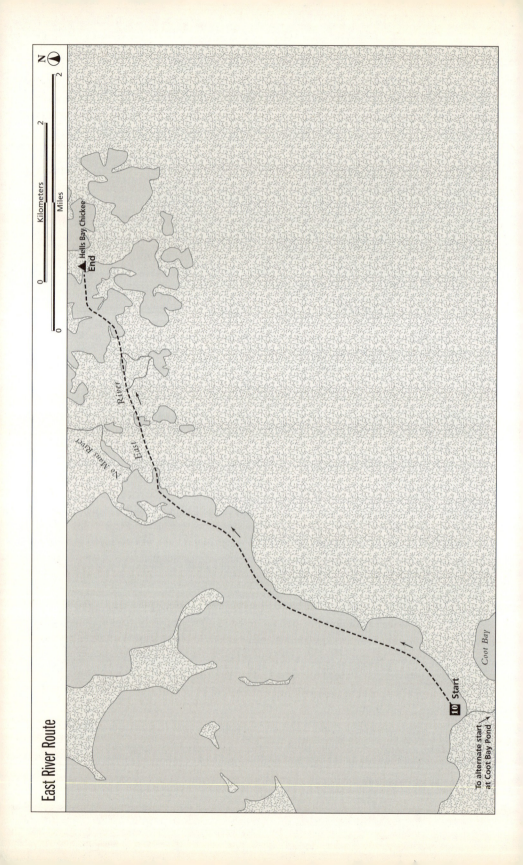

extend higher on either side of the channel. Due to the trees, the wind may not be a factor; however, the tide can be against you. The river will run due east for the most part, with smaller creeks funneling off and small bays. A smaller creek connects to No Mans River, veering off to the left.

The river makes a few turns and then turns north, running about 50 to 60 feet wide. You will come to a bay with two narrow outlets. The smaller channel, on the left, heads north. Take the river to the right, heading east-northeast for about 0.25 mile. The waterway then divides for a second time, both creeks leading to Hells Bay.

Enter the Gates of Hell on an eastern course, passing between two mangrove islets. About 200 yards ahead is a marker, the last one on the Hells Bay Canoe Trail. From here to the main park road, the canoe trail is 6.0 miles.

Continue paddling east to the PVC marker; Hells Bay Chickee is on your right.

Option: Lane Bay Chickee is an additional 2.0 miles heading north and slightly west through Wells Bay, threading your way through mangroves.

36 Joe River Route

Joe River veers off to the northwest around Whitewater Bay This southern river provides an alternative route to the other side of the bay, without all the waves and boat traffic. Great for beginners, this route is also great for fishing and camping. Joe River starts out wide like a bay and then narrows down into a river. This route makes up two loops—one around Whitewater Bay, the other around Cape Sable.

County: Monroe
Start: Marker 10, Whitewater Bay. Launch from the Coot Bay ramp off the main Everglades National Park Road. Paddle to Tarpon Creek and then to Whitewater Bay.
End: Joe River Chickee
Distance: 12.0 miles one-way
Approximate float time: All day
Difficulty: Mild to moderate paddling
Nearest town: Flamingo
Season: Fall, winter, and early spring
Fees: Park entrance fee
Highlights: Fishing, mangroves, camping
Hazards: Powerboats on river
Campsites: Joe River Chickee
Getting there: To launch from Coot Bay Pond (adding a few extra miles and time), enter Everglades National Park from Homestead heading south and west and follow the main park road (FL 9336) 30 miles to Coot Bay Pond. Paddle up to the launch site at Marker 10 and continue from there. Paddle north and west toward Coot Bay. Paddle through Coot Bay looking for the Tarpon Creek pass. Through this small lake you will see a few markers along the way 3, 4 Markers, and then 8 will lead you into Tarpon Creek.

As you come out of Tarpon Creek near Marker 10, the water will be about 4 feet deep. It will get a little deeper through the open bay. Look north and slightly west for your markers. Watching boat traffic can be a benefit—you can follow their lead. Stay to the right of their path and you will be able to paddle with less interference.

Paddle between a few islands and continue heading north and west to Marker 18. You have traveled 3.0 miles since Marker 10. You will be

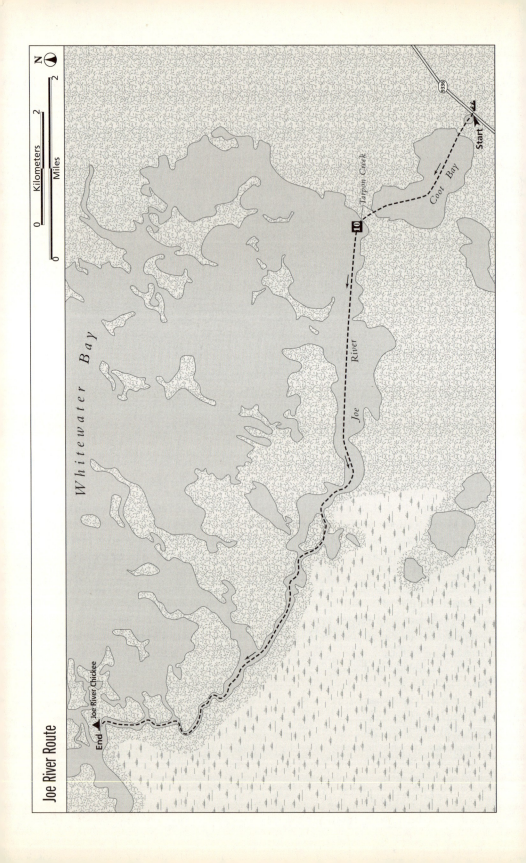

in open water through this bay, Whitewater. You might also arrange for a powerboat shuttle out to the start point.

The Paddle

This internal route in Whitewater Bay could be an all-day trip or part of a multiday adventure.

Starting from Marker 10, at the entrance of Whitewater Bay from Tarpon Creek, head west into the large bay. (There may or may not be markers in this.) Stay near the left shore to help navigate your way into Joe River.

Continue paddling west through the bay, which narrows. The waterway resembles more of a river around Mile 5, although the waterway will still be about 200 feet across. The depth will vary depending on the season, maybe 5 to 6 feet. Mangroves from 4 to 40 feet tall flank the river on large islands, or keys. Due to its depth, the river is a popular route for powerboats. Watch for the manatee warning sign.

Continue paddling, heading southwest along the shore. Watch for a channel heading off to the left, which leads around a mangrove island to South Joe River Chickee. Paddle around a few twists and turns and come to the chickee, ahead in the bay. The chickee is a double, great for families. You have paddled 6.0 miles.

Leaving the chickee, swing around and head up the creek you didn't come in on. Follow this creek north, back to the main river. Joe River meanders northwest and bends around to the left. Up ahead, a large mangrove island splits the river. You can paddle on either side; however, the right side is recommended. The river is still fairly wide here.

Continue paddling around the mangroves and along the shore. You may see some feeder streams on the sides. Soon the river turns in a northward direction. As you paddle through, you will notice three separate channels that lead off to your right and head into Whitewater Bay. You will have awesome views of the bay from the channels. Joe River Chickee, at mile 12.0, is the end of this route.

Option: Oyster Bay Chickee is 4.0 miles farther through the Cormorant Pass Route.

37 Middle Cape Route

This voyage takes you along shores whose human history dates back to the Native Americans and also offers shell-surfing opportunities. Along this route are gumbo-limbo trees and cabbage palms, as well as a variety of grasses in lieu of the tangle of mangroves you often find yourself crawling under, around, and through when paddling the Everglades. Other highlights include the historic site of Fort Cross, dating back to 1850s, great birding along Lake Ingraham, and the opportunity to see a variety of ecosystems.

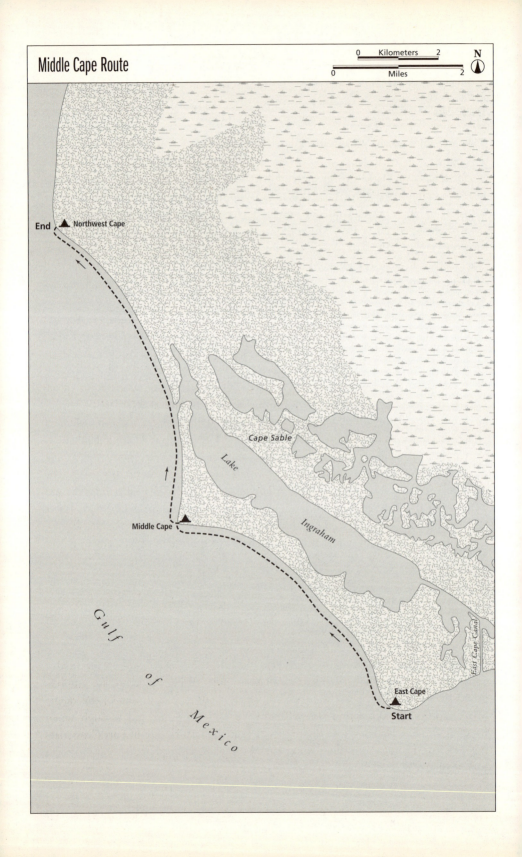

County: Monroe
Launch: East Cape campsite
End: Northwest Cape campsite
Distance: 9.5 miles one-way
Approximate float time: 5 hours
Difficulty: Mild to moderate paddling
Nearest town: Flamingo
Season: Fall, winter, and early spring
Fees: Park entrance fee
Highlights: Beaches and beach camping

Hazards: Waves and tide
Campsites: East, Middle, and Northwest Capes
Connectors: East Cape and Big Sable Routes
Getting there: Coming from Homestead, the entrance to Everglades National Park is off CR 997 (Krome Avenue), which is off US 1. Go through the main gate onto FL 9336, follow the main road all the way down, 38 miles to Flamingo, and launch from there.

The Paddle

As part of a multiday trip, you could paddle northwest and camp or start at Northwest Cape and paddle southeast back to Flamingo. If you want to start from Northwest Cape, consider arranging a powerboat shuttle.

Cape Sable offers natural vegetation and miles of shell-surfing beaches. There were coconut farms and harvesting in this area from the late 1800s until the early 1930s. The tide may get stronger as you near the Gulf, and the ecosystem will change to beautiful prairies, strands of Jamaica dogwood, and wooded hammocks.

From East Cape campsite, head northwest into the Gulf. As you paddle, you will see Middle Cape on your left as you round the East Cape. As the beach narrows, the shoreline is resplendent with grasses and a variety of trees, including gumbo-limbo and cabbage palms—a welcome respite from miles of mangroves. The beach runs along the shoreline all the way to Middle Cape. Continue paddling and come to prairies with palms and cactus.

Following the shoreline, veer west to Middle Cape, at 4.5 miles. A point here was once the site of Fort Cross, dating back to the 1850s and used as a base by U.S. soldiers in the government's attempt to eradicate Seminoles. Past this point, the coast recommences a north–south compass reading. In the late 1800s a coconut farm—Waddell Plantation—was established around Middle Cape. Coconuts were harvested here on and off until the palms were devastated by a hurricane in 1935.

Paddle past Middle Cape at 6.0 miles. This waterway connects Lake Ingraham with the Gulf, and the tides here can be strong. Mangroves flank the shore, rising out of the sand to welcome you to one of the most beautiful oases on Florida's east coast. You will see a palm prairie as you paddle northwest. The prairie goes back a ways. The ecosystem here includes some wooded hammocks, cactus, and Jamaica dogwood. This habitat traverses to Northwest Cape and beyond.

Continue paddling through the open water until you come to the very appealing Northwest Cape campsite.

Options: From here it is 6.0 miles north to Shark River Island, using the Big Sable Route.

If the wind is too strong around Middle Cape, there is another possible route from East Cape to Northwest Cape. However, this route depends on the tidal current and can be impassable due to low water. This is a great birding trail (Lake Ingraham) as well.

As you paddle away from East Cape on an easterly course, paddle to the East Cape Canal. Turn left (north) into the canal, which can be difficult if the tide is coming out. Head toward the dam and the Old Homestead Canal (part of the Bear Lake Canoe Trail). Before you reach the dam, turn left (northwest) and paddle through a canal into Lake Ingraham. From here you can follow the markers across the shallow lake and do some bird watching.

Continue paddling, heading northwest across the lake to Middle Cape Canal, if that's your destination. Be careful to watch the tide—you might get trapped in the lake if you don't head out with the tide. Watch for powerboats on the lake. They won't slow down for you, else they also get caught by the tide.

To continue on the Northwest Cape, head north along Little Sable Creek from Lake Ingraham. This creek will most likely be overgrown with vegetation. Reenter the Gulf slightly north of the Northwest Cape campsite.

38 Broad River Route

NOTE: This route was closed in 2007 due to hurricane damage. Check with the ENP Gulf Coast Ranger Station for current status before heading out.

This waterway offers a variety of plants and routes. In addition to oyster bars, you will also need to maneuver around islands on this route. Broad River, as its name implies, is very wide at certain points—up to 230 feet across. It is wider where it meets the Wilderness Waterway. The river intersects a connecting river for alternate routes that also lead to campsites. You will encounter mangroves, gumbo-limbo trees, palms, poisonwood, and Brazilian pepper. The Park Service is struggling to remove this invasive plant; however, birds eat the berries and keep spreading the seeds around.

County: Monroe
Start: Gulf Coast, near mouth of Broad River, partly on the Wilderness Waterway. (This route is on the Gulf side of the Everglades, near Highland Beach Chickee.)
End: Camp Lonesome
Distance: 11.5 miles one-way (add approximately 24 miles more when launching from Chokoloskee)

Approximate float time: 5 to 6-plus hours, or a multiday paddle; a good rule of thumb is about 2-3 miles per hour, when paddling.
Difficulty: Moderate to difficult paddling
Nearest town: Chokoloskee/Everglades City; Flamingo also accessible
Season: Fall, winter, and spring
Fees: Park entrance fee; powerboat shuttle; if coming from Chokoloskee, boat ramp fee

Highlights: Varied ecosystems and vegetation, fishing
Hazards: Powerboats, tide on Broad River, tide, current on open waterways
Campsites: Highland Beach Chickee, Broad River, Camp Lonesome
Connectors: Highland Beach, Wood River, the Nightmare, Cabbage Island Shortcut, Rodgers River Bay
Getting there: Coming from Homestead, the entrance to Everglades National Park is off CR 997 (Krome Avenue), which is off US 1. Go through the main gate onto FL 9336, follow the main road all the way down, 38 miles to Flamingo, and launch from there. The distance is shorter coming from Chokoloskee Causeway.
To get to Chokoloskee, on the Naples side: Take FL 29 south from US 41 (Tamiami Trial) about 7 miles. You can park along the causeway to launch or launch from the ramp at Outdoor Resorts, possible fee (239-695-3788).

From either location, you may want to hire a shuttle to transport you, or the paddle can be arduous.

From Chokoloskee Causeway, paddle south and east, following the mainland around toward Rabbit Key (5.5 miles), but keeping closer to the mainland. Continue paddling southeast toward Crate Key and then on to Pavilion Key, which will be on the outside, on your right. Continue paddling between islands, such as Duck Rock Cove and Gun Rock, heading toward Mormon Key past Huston and Chatham River bays. Paddle further southeast to New Turkey and Turkey campsites (islands), then passing North Plover Key, Plover Key, Bird Key, Boggess Point, Wood Key, Hog Key campsite, Hog Key, Lostmans Key (and River), to Highland Beach and Chickee.

The Paddle

This route can be part of a multiday paddle from either Flamingo or Chockolosee, or you can arrange for a powerboat shuttle from either town to the entrance of Broad River, south of the Highland Beach Chickee.

Along this route you will paddle from salt water in the Gulf of Mexico into freshwater on the Broad River.

From the Gulf follow the markers and enter the Broad River. Watch out for oyster bars along the way. Low tides and oyster bars make this a risky route for powerboats. The bay contains several islands to maneuver around. Stay to the east and try not to enter the Rodgers River. The Broad River is very wide—at times more than 230 feet across—and wider where it meets with the Wilderness Watery (Marker 25).

The Wood River and the Nightmare intersect with the Broad River. The Wood River route goes east for about 10.0 miles to Camp Lonesome. The Nightmare route goes south 8.5 miles to the Harney River Chickee. East of Marker 25 on the Broad River is Broad River campsite (2.0 miles from the Gulf). There is a dock here, and the site is good for both camping and picnicking. You may encounter strong tides while paddling upriver.

Resume paddling on the Broad River, heading northeast along shores lined with gumbo-limbos, palms, poisonwood, Brazilian pepper, and mangroves.

Continue paddling until you reach the Cutoff, after a sharp curve in the river, about 6.0 miles from your starting point. The Cutoff is at the north side of the bend,

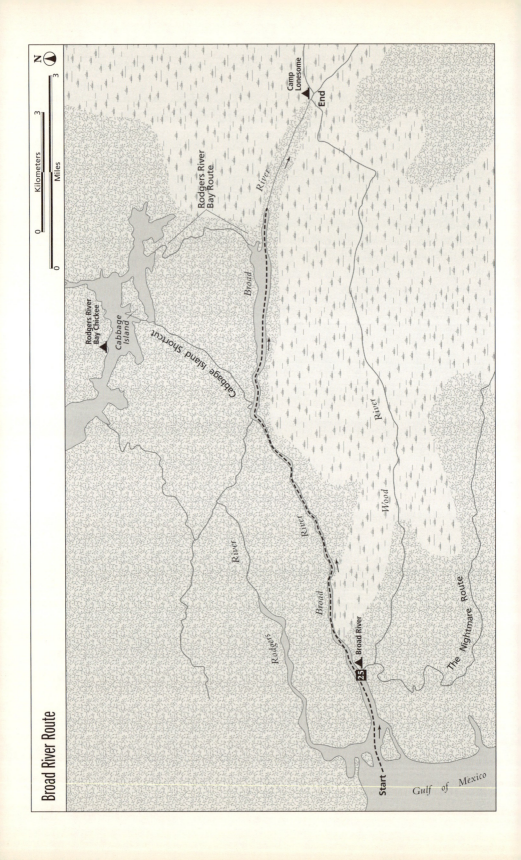

which connects to Rodgers River. About 150 yards farther east is the Cabbage Island Shortcut, which can take you to Rodgers River Bay.

Past the mangroves and buttonwoods, about a 0.5 mile east of the Cutoff, the Broad River narrows before entering the bay. Paddle along the bay until Marker 26, where you will come to the Wilderness Waterway, 8.5 miles from your starting point. The Wilderness Waterway heads north toward Rodgers River Bay Chickee, which lies about 4.0 miles ahead. Stay on the Broad River, which continues to wind its way east toward Camp Lonesome.

As you continue paddling east, the river narrows again and you come to an island in the middle of the waterway. After going around the island, the river broadens. You will pass a water monitoring station on the left bank. The waters here are usually fresh and clear, and the river is about 50 feet across. Interspersed with the mangroves, palms and wax myrtles languidly reach out across the water.

The Wood River flows in from your right and an unnamed channel comes in from the opposite direction. The Broad River meets up from the left, creating a confluence of these three waterways plus the bay you are on.

Turn left and head up the Broad River past gumbo-limbos, Jamaica dogwood, and mangroves. Continue on this route until you reach Camp Lonesome, its dock hidden around trees and brush. This is 11.5 miles from your start point and the end of this route. On this little island there used to be a shell mound made by the Calusa and Seminole Indians.

Option: The Wood River heads west about 10.0 miles and rejoins the Broad River at the Nightmare.

39 Shark Cutoff Route

This route is mainly a connector from Tarpon Bay, along the Shark River, and down to Oyster Bay (or a reverse route). You will be following the mangroves and buttonwoods along this waterway as it meets up with the Wilderness Waterway. Be sure to bring a compass and chart to help you navigate—you may feel a little overwhelmed among the mangroves in the confluence of rivers meeting and branching off to the sides. You will pass a few chickees along the way where you can stop and stretch.

County: Monroe
Start: Tarpon Bay; Marker 9, Wilderness Waterway, via Coot Bay Pond, Whitewater Bay
End: Oyster Bay Chickee
Distance: 7.5 miles one-way (additional 3+ miles from Coot Bay Pond launch)

Approximate float time: 3 hours (add 1 to 2 hours from Coot Bay Pond)
Difficulty: Easy to moderate paddling
Nearest town: Flamingo
Season: Fall, winter, and early spring
Fees: Park entrance fee

Highlights: Trees, marked trail, Wilderness Waterway
Hazards: Tides
Campsites: Shark River Chickee, Oyster Bay Chickee
Getting there: Coming from Homestead, the entrance to Everglades National Park is off CR 997 (Krome Avenue), which is off US 1. Go through the main gate onto FL 9336. To launch from Coot Bay Pond (adding a few extra miles and time), enter Everglades National Park from Homestead heading south and west, and follow the main park road (FL 9336) 30 miles to Coot Bay Pond.

Paddle north and west toward Coot Bay. Paddle through Coot Bay looking for the Tarpon Creek pass. Through this small lake you will see a few markers along the way, 3, 4, 8, and 9; this will lead you into Tarpon Creek.

As you come out of Tarpon Creek near Marker 10, the water will be about 4 feet deep. It will get a little deeper through the open bay. Look north and slightly west for your markers. Watching boat traffic can be a benefit—you can follow their lead. Stay to the right of their path and you will be able to paddle with less interference.

Paddle between a few islands and continue heading north and west to Marker 18. You have traveled 3.0 miles since Marker 10. Paddle northeast for a strait between a series of islands (keys) following the markers up to 40, through Whitewater Bay. From here (Marker 40), it gets a little tricky, but you want to maneuver between the mangroves, paddling northwest, up to Oyster Bay, where you jump from Marker 48 to 2, at the southern part of Oyster Bay. Paddle north up to Shark Cutoff Route, Marker 5, then turning 90 degrees to the right and following Little Shark River. Paddle due east on Little Shark River, past the chickee, Marker 6. Continue to Marker 8 where you will need to turn almost 90 degrees left, heading north. This will take you to Marker 9, on the Wilderness Waterway.

The Paddle

This is an internal route in Whitewater Bay and can be part of a multiday trip.

This paddle begins in the Wilderness Waterway, 4.0 miles west of Canepatch campsite. Follow the mangroves and buttonwoods along the Shark River, heading south. Paddle toward the taller mangroves in the distance until you reach the Wilderness Waterway at Marker 9, 2.0 miles downriver. An unnamed channel (from the right) coming in from Tarpon Bay is an alternate route to Canepatch campsite. The Shark River broadens here as it turns to the west.

Continue paddling downriver, absorbing nature at its finest, and soon pass Gunboat Island, a rather large island. You have paddled 3.5 miles. As you paddle around the island, you will come to a water-monitoring station. Encircled by mangroves, the Shark River, and Little Shark, you will feel like you are in a forest with little or no civilization.

Reach another no-name channel, which can take you south to the Labyrinth. To your west is the Shark River. Continue straight ahead on the Little Shark River.

Paddle southwest toward the Wilderness Waterway. The Graveyard Creek route, to the north, meets up with Graveyard Creek, about 7.0 miles to the west. Continue paddling southwest on the Little Shark River, which narrows after the confluence of the rivers. You will soon come to the Shark River Chickee, at the next channel, and

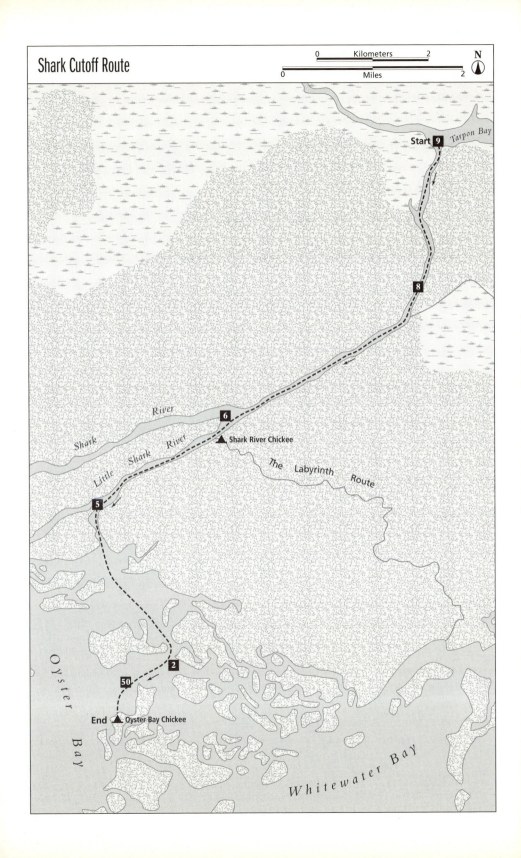

the beginning of the Labyrinth Route. The chickee, about 50 yards down the channel and 4.5 miles from your launch, is a great place to stretch or camp. There is no dry ground here or along the route; however, a long-term drought has made the water shallower than normal.

Depart the chickee and head back to the Little Shark River. Paddle southwest on the Wilderness Waterway for about 1.5 miles to Marker 5. Here you will meet up with the Shark Cutoff. Circle around and head south on the waterway, navigating the winding creek into the northern border of Oyster Bay. Use this bay to head southeast to an access between mangrove islands. Although it may appear to be one long island, it is not. Continue paddling through a pass between the islands and look for Marker 2.

Leave the Wilderness Waterway here and head southwest toward Marker 50. **DO NOT** follow these markers or you will end up in Cormorant Pass. Continue paddling south toward another group of islands. Surrounded by these mangrove islands, the Oyster Bay Chickee sits inside a lagoon. You have paddled at least 7.5 miles from your start point.

Option: From here it is 4.0 miles south to the Joe River via the Cormorant Pass.

Florida Bay

Paddling in Florida Bay is often difficult due to wind, tide, shallow basins, motorized boats, and the need for navigational skills. Treacherous passes cut through long banks of mud and sea grass, which separate the shallow basins. Be sure to carry a compass and a weatherproof chart to aid in navigation. Recommended charts include NOAA chart 11451, Ten Thousand Islands charts 11430 and 11432, and Whitewater Bay chart 11433. The shallow areas are not always marked. Remember the boaters rhyme (see page 13).

40 West Lake to Alligator Creek

NOTE: West Lake is closed to vessels with motors greater than 5.5 horsepower. Motors are prohibited from the east end of West Lake to Garfield Bight. This route is not recommended on windy days due to exposed, rough waters. Guides are available for this route from the Everglades Hostel.

West Lake was popular for hunting and fishing from 1916 until the 1930s, and alligator and plume hunters used this trail to access creeks and lakes for their wildlife. Those wishing to overnight may camp at Alligator Creek and then return to West Lake or head into Florida Bay to Flamingo. With mosquitoes your constant companions, you'll paddle through a series of large open lakes connected by narrow creeks lined with mangroves. The diversity makes this a fun route to paddle. Before Hurricanes Wilma and Katrina, it was not uncommon to see a flock of flamingos in this area. Today you can still see many of the wading birds found in other areas of the Everglades.

County: Miami-Dade
Start/End: Dock in West Lake, Everglades National Park, on the main park road coming from Ernest F. Coe Visitor Center or up from Flamingo
Distance: 8.5 miles one-way to Alligator Creek; 17.0 miles round-trip
Approximate float time: All-day
Difficulty: Mild to moderate paddling
Nearest town: Flamingo
Season: Fall, winter, and early spring
Fees: Park entrance fee; permit required for overnight camping

Highlights: No motorboat traffic; alligators and crocodiles
Hazards: Downed trees, wind, rough waters
Campsites: Alligator Creek, Shark Point
Getting there: Coming from Homestead, the entrance to Everglades National Park is off CR 997 (Krome Avenue), which is off US 1. Go through the main gate onto FL 9336 and follow the main road past Nine Mile Pond (at 25 miles) and Hells Bay to West Lake canoe launch on your left.

The Paddle

Launch from the dock in West Lake and head south into the main lake. Follow the shore to the south and then to the east. Occasional markers in the water will help guide you. There is a creek that takes you from West Lake to Long Lake. As you paddle into this narrow waterway, maybe 12 feet wide, you will be shaded by branches.

The creek opens up into Long Lake, which can be shallow at certain times of year. Paddle around the small islands, heading south on the eastern side of the lake to the entrance of Mangrove Creek.

Mangrove Creek runs between two small lakes and continues through a shady red mangrove area. You will also see the roots (pneumatophores) of black mangroves. All

West Lake to Alligator Creek

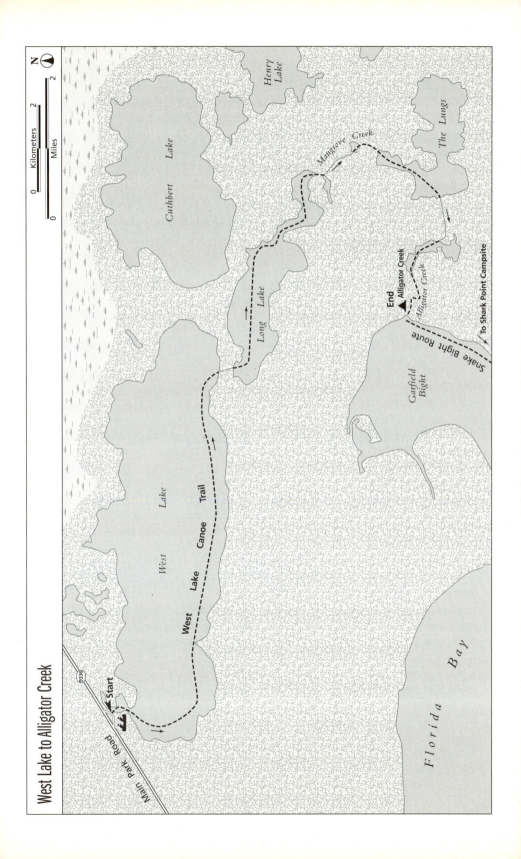

mangroves produce small white or yellow flowers, which can be pollinated by moths, bees, wasps, and even the wind.

Paddle over the mangrove prop roots. Keep heading southeast down the creek into the Lungs, so named because this body of water vaguely resembles the shape of human lungs. Enter this cove, heading south, and go into the main part of the lake. You will see markers for Alligator Creek on the west shore. If you look up into the mangroves, you may see dozens of brown pelicans looking down at you. They are almost like guerrilla sentries.

Tracks or markings from alligators can be seen along the shore, hence the creek's name. This is a wide waterway, with mangroves lining the shores. As you paddle you will pass through a few small ponds before coming to an open prairie behind scattered black mangrove trees.

After the prairie you will pass the remnants of an old road bridge. The bridge was built during the 1930s and used by government employees who were trying to remove tree cotton. Native to the Everglades, tree cotton was considered blighted and considered a threat by commercial cotton operators. After the bridge pilings you will come to Alligator Creek campsite. Here is Garfield Bight, part of Florida Bay. You have paddled about 8.5 miles from your launch site, and here is where the trail ends.

Option: Shark Point campsite is about 2.5 miles farther via the Snake Bight Route.

41 Snake Bight Route

This route is actually an extension of the West Lake to Alligator Creek route. On this great multiday adventure, you will come face-to-face with different habitats and environments inside the Everglades. You will encounter alligators, crocodiles, and possibly shallow, muddy water and wind along this route. Guides are available from the Everglades International Hostel.

County: Miami-Dade
Start: Alligator Creek campsite
End: Flamingo
Distance: 8.5 miles from West Lake canoe launch to Alligator Creek Campsite, then 12 miles to Flamingo
Approximate float time: All day
Difficulty: Moderate paddling
Nearest town: Flamingo
Season: Fall, winter and early spring
Fees: Park entrance fee
Highlights: Wildlife, Florida Bay

Hazards: Alligators, crocodiles, shallow water, winds on the bay
Campsites: Alligator Creek
Getting there: Coming from Homestead, the entrance to Everglades National Park is off CR 997 (Krome Avenue), which is off US 1. Go through the main gate onto FL 9336 and follow the main road past Nine Mile Pond (25 miles down) and Hells Bay to West Lake canoe launch on your left. Launch from the dock in West Lake and head south into the main lake. Follow the shore to the south and then to the

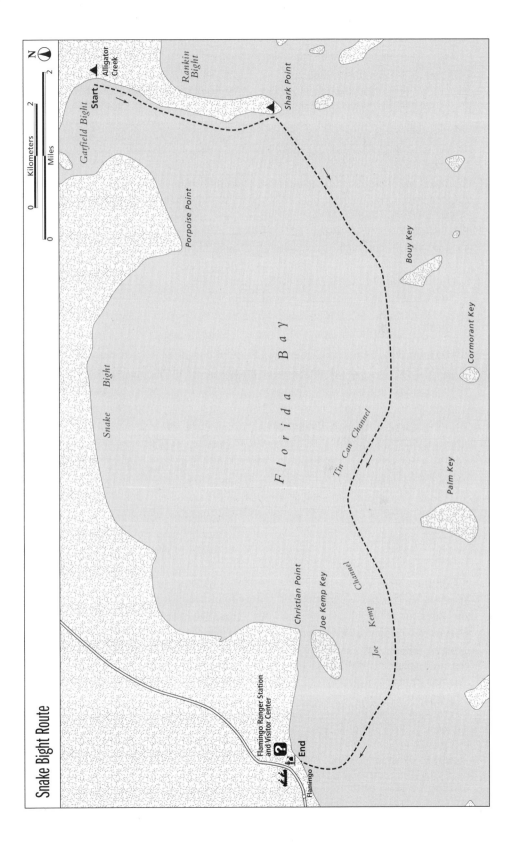

east. Occasional markers in the water will help guide you. There is a creek that takes you from West Lake to Long Lake. As you paddle into this narrow waterway, maybe 12 feet wide, you will be shaded by branches.

The creek opens up into Long Lake, which can be shallow at certain times of year. Paddle around the small islands, heading south on the eastern side of the lake to the entrance of Mangrove Creek.

Mangrove Creek runs between two small lakes and continues through a shady red mangrove area. Paddle over the mangrove prop roots. Keep heading southeast down the creek into the Lungs, so named because this body of water vaguely resembles the shape of human lungs. Enter this cove, heading south, and go into the main part of the lake. You will see markers for Alligator Creek on the west shore.

This is a wide waterway, with mangroves lining the shores. As you paddle you will pass through a few small ponds before coming to an open prairie behind scattered black mangrove trees.

After the prairie you will pass the remnants of an old road bridge. After the bridge pilings you will come to Alligator Creek campsite. Here is Garfield Bight, part of Florida Bay. You have paddled about 8.5 miles from your launch site.

The Paddle

Leave Alligator Creek campsite and head south. Paddle along the left (east) bank, along Garfield Bight. The bottom of this waterway is muddy, making the water brown. Pass a water-monitoring station and you will see the Flamingo tower to the west in the distance beyond Porpoise Point.

Continue paddling south along the creek to Shark Point. There may be a small beach area here where you can pull up and stretch before your "open-water" paddle across the bay. From here you can head west across Snake Bight if you have a good tide. However, if the wind and tide are heading out, this area will be mostly mud and you will be dragging your canoe or kayak.

Instead continue paddling on a southwesterly course toward Bouy Key. If the tide is going out (west), this will aid in your paddling across the bay. The water will also be deeper here. At the northern tip of Bouy Key, you have gone 4.5 miles. From here you will take the Tin Can Channel west.

Continue paddling through this channel, through Florida Bay and past Cormorant and Palm Keys. Paddle around the outside of Joe Kemp Key to avoid the shallow water. From here, head north across Joe Kemp Channel and paddle west of the marked bird-nesting island to enter the cut to Flamingo. You should be able to see the visitor center.

42 Florida Bay Loop

NOTE: Carl Ross Key campsite is currently closed to overnight camping and only available for day use.

This excursion will take you to Little Rabbit Key and return to Flamingo. You will paddle approximately 36.0 miles on this **multiday adventure** as you head west and circle around several islands and head to Sandy and Carl Ross Keys. This area, a significant nesting area for roseate spoonbills, was heavily damaged by Hurricanes Katrina and Wilma.

County: Monroe (Florida Bay)
Start: Flamingo Bay Marina
End: Carl Ross Key
Distance: Approximately 36.0 miles one-way
Approximate float time: 2 to 3 days
Difficulty: Moderate to difficult paddling
Nearest town: Flamingo
Season: Fall, winter, and early spring
Fees: Park entrance fee
Highlights: Wildlife

Hazards: Winds, strong tide, motorboat traffic
Campsites: Little Rabbit Key (**NOTE:** The Park Service may replace Carl Ross Key campsite.)
Getting there: Coming from Homestead, the entrance to Everglades National Park is off CR 997 (Krome Avenue), which is off US 1. Go through the main gate onto FL 9336, follow the main road 38 miles down to the marina, and launch from here.

The Paddle

After checking with the park ranger regarding tide, weather, etc., and obtaining overnight permits, launch from Flamingo. Paddle southwest and head for Bradley Key. Stay to the southeast of the tip of Bradley Key; you will be paddling beyond here to reach First National Bank. The water will be shallow until you pass the key.

After you reach Bradley Key, look for marker number eight near Oyster Keys; stay west. Proceed to Marker 6 and paddle between here and Conchie Channel. As you pass here, you will soon be able to see Carl Ross and Sandy Keys ahead. Stay west until you see the marked Rocky Channel, where you want to turn south. Keep an eye on the tides—this channel may be shallow as you near the key. Paddle carefully into this protected rookery.

The former campsite is 10.0 miles from the Flamingo launch site. Return to Flamingo, or paddle farther to camp at Little Rabbit Key for the night.

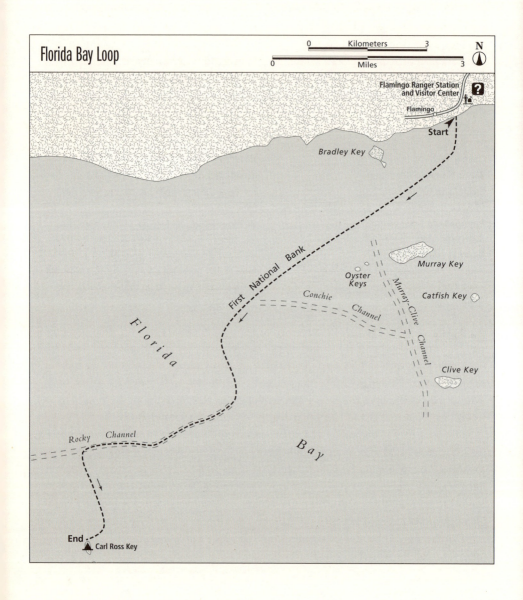

43 Carl Ross Key to Little Rabbit Key (via Man of War Key)

NOTE: There is another Rabbit Key up near Chokoloskee. Don't confuse that one with this Florida Bay route.

This route affords great birding. However, you will also encounter shallow water and, at times, stronger tides. This route is all open water, with no place to stop along the way. If the winds pick up, you will need to keep your heading so that you don't drift too far away from the mainland or the islands. Time your trip to launch with the outgoing tide and return with the incoming tide.

County: Monroe (Florida Bay)
Start: Carl Ross Key
End: Little Rabbit Key
Distance: Approximately 13.0 miles one-way
Approximate float time: 6 hours
Difficulty: Moderate to difficult paddling
Nearest town: Flamingo
Season: Fall, winter, and spring
Fees: Park entrance fee

Highlights: Open water, a variety of birds, possibly dolphins
Hazards: Strong tides and winds
Campsites: Little Rabbit Key
Getting there: Coming from Homestead, the entrance to Everglades National Park is off CR 997 (Krome Avenue), which is off US 1. Go through the main gate onto FL 9336, follow the main road 38 miles to the marina at Flamingo, and launch from here.

The Paddle

You can paddle this multiday trip in its entirety or arrange a powerboat shuttle from the marina to Carl Ross Key.

As you paddle away from Carl Ross Key, head south past Sandy Key and then paddle east toward Man of War Key. The water around First National Bank will be shallow unless the tides are coming in. This will all be open water as you head south and then east.

Paddle past Man of War Channel (6.0 miles from your start point); you may encounter strong currents here. At Man of War Key, stay south and keep the island to the north; it will be shallow around here. Once you paddle past this point, you might be able to see Rabbit Keys off in the distance to the southeast. The larger island on your left is Big Rabbit Key; the smaller isle on your right is Little Rabbit.

As you paddle across Rabbit Key Basin, the water should be deeper and clear with a grassy bottom. On Little Rabbit Key the dock is on the west side, facing you. This quiet campsite away from civilization will amaze you.

Option: Combine this paddle with the Little Rabbit Key to Flamingo route to loop back up to Flamingo.

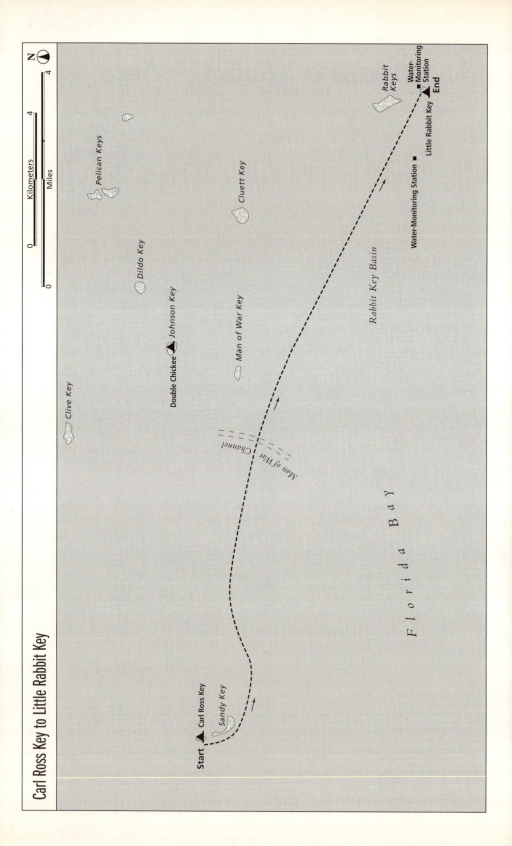

44 Little Rabbit Key to Flamingo

This route will be a little challenging, depending on the wind and tide. You want to time your paddle with the tide coming back in. This route has various detours along the way of small keys interspersed in the bay. From here you have two choices: Go around the east side of Big Rabbit Key and follow the shoreline north past several islands; or go back into Rabbit Basin, up along the marsh to Cluett Key, and through the pass.

County: Monroe (Florida Bay)
Start: Little Rabbit Key campsite
End: Flamingo marina
Distance: 12.5 miles one-way
Approximate float time: 6 hours
Difficulty: Moderate paddling
Nearest town: Flamingo
Season: Fall, winter, and early spring
Fees: Park entrance fee

Highlights: Birds, fish, wildlife
Hazards: Strong winds, tides, motorboat traffic
Campsites: Little Rabbit Key
Getting there: Coming from Homestead, the entrance to Everglades National Park is off CR 997 (Krome Avenue), which is off US 1. Go through the main gate onto FL 9336, follow the main road 38 miles to the marina at Flamingo, and launch from here.

There are a few interpretive signs along various routes. This one depicts some of the birds that are common at Mrazek Pond in the Everglades.

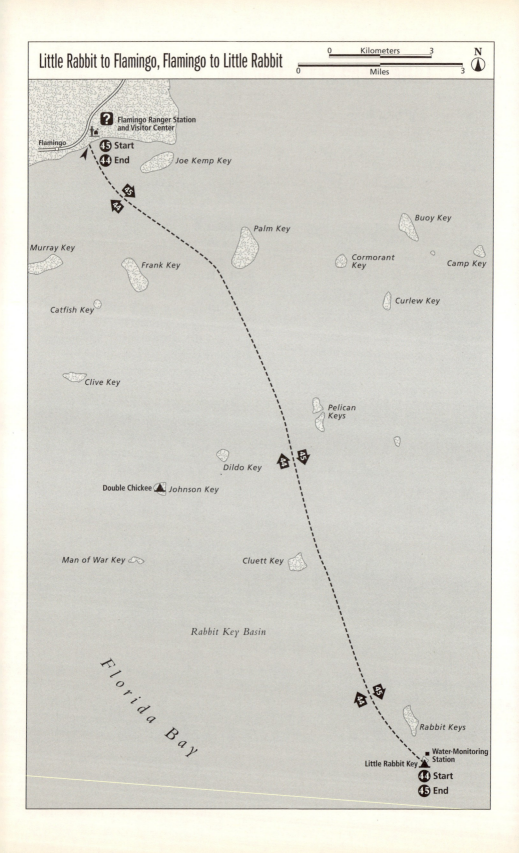

The Paddle

This is an internal route in Florida Bay. You can paddle this as multiday trip in its entirety or arrange a powerboat shuttle from the marina to Little Rabbit Key.

For this route you will go along the west side of Florida Bay and through Rabbit Key Basin. Leave the campsite and paddle north around Big Rabbit Key. Head toward Cluett Key, 4.0 miles north, which will be on the east side. The water here is deeper than on the north or east sides of Dildo Key Bank, and the tide flows in an east–west direction. As you paddle up to Cluett Key, you should be able to see through the channel to the east side of Dildo Key.

Paddle around the marsh, heading east and then north. Come around the tip and head west toward the Pelican Keys. The water may be shallow in this area, so paddle closer to the twin Pelican Keys as you head northwest toward Flamingo. This whole route is mostly open water, and although a chart and compass are always necessary, you shouldn't need to keep looking at them to stay on course. This route also has land and campsites you can use for directional purposes.

Option: If you're feeling up to it, a short 1.5-mile side trip will take you to Catfish Key—another great area with a profusion of birdlife. Watch for motorboats as you paddle from Pelican Keys or Catfish Key back to Flamingo, following the channel markers home.

45 Flamingo to Little Rabbit Key

Check with the park ranger regarding tide, weather, and overnight permits before heading out. You will begin by heading south to southeast toward Frank Key, where there are usually a lot of nesting birds. This route also passes Joe Kemp Key (heavy motorized boat traffic) and Dildo Key Bank, named for a cactus. You can either continue south along the larger islands or head west through Cluett Pass. You may choose to explore Rabbit Key Basin along the way for birding or to stop and stretch.

County: Monroe, Florida Bay
Start: Flamingo marina
End: Little Rabbit Key
Distance: Approximately 12.5 miles one-way
Approximate float time: 6 hours
Difficulty: Moderate to difficult paddling
Nearest town: Flamingo
Season: Fall, winter, and spring
Fees: Park entrance fee

Highlights: Birds and fish
Hazards: Motorboat traffic, strong tides, wind
Campsites: Little Rabbit Key
Getting there: Coming from Homestead, the entrance to Everglades National Park is off CR 997 (Krome Avenue), which is off US 1. Go through the main gate onto FL 9336, follow the main road 38 miles to the marina at Flamingo, and launch from here.

The Paddle

This is an internal route in Florida Bay. You can paddle this as a multiday trip in its entirety or arrange a powerboat shuttle from the marina to Little Rabbit Key.

Launch from Flamingo and head south-southeast (maybe 140 degrees) toward Frank Key, with Palm Key on your left. You will pass Joe Kemp Key as you head into the heavily trafficked boat area. Near Frank Key you will see a great deal of birds, which nest in many of these mangrove islands. You may also see ospreys near Flamingo.

This area is mostly shallow flats, with motes around the islands. On the other side of Frank Key is a smaller island called Catfish Key—a possible side trip that will add another 1.5 miles to your trip.

Continue paddling south-southeast as you will pass along the east side of Dildo Key Bank. The water may be a little deeper, but overall it is relatively shallow through this route. Dildo Key is named for a cactus that's indigenous to Florida. It has three stems and is thorny, similar to the shape of this island. Dildo Key has several keys around the perimeter and a few channels you can use to paddle around the island. Paddling along the east side of Dildo Key, you will come to the twin Pelican Keys on your left. Proceed between the islands and the land. The water is likely to be shallow here, so it may be better to stay closer to Pelican Keys.

Keep paddling south around the island, Pelican Keys. Depending on the tide, time of day, and how tired you are, you can elect to turn and go west toward Cluett Key, following the outline of Dildo Key, or continue paddling south and slightly east to the next larger landmass. The water past this inlet should be a little deeper as you head around the land and south to the Rabbit Keys campsite. The tide around this area should have an east–west direction.

You can explore Rabbit Key Basin—bird watching, etc. —or paddle north inside the basin, following the west shore of Big Rabbit Key up to Cluett Key, which is 4.0 miles from Little Rabbit Key.

You may be able to take a pass or cut through here to the east side of Dildo Key and return to Flamingo the way you came down. Or you can launch from Little Rabbit Key and reverse your paddle back to Flamingo.

Option: For an alternative route back to Flamingo, paddle west across Rabbit Key Basin. As you come out of the pass, turn right and follow the shoreline. Then paddle north to Man of War Channel and take this pass northward, following the west shoreline of Dildo Key. Pass Johnson Key platform on your right and continue paddling around Clive Key at the northern tip of Dildo Key. After you pass through here, head north and east toward Catfish and Frank Keys, the way you came out from Flamingo. This route is definitely longer; however, you may have more wildlife (birds and fish) to enjoy.

46 The Wilderness Waterway

This route is 99.0 miles one-way on an inland water route between Flamingo and Gulf Coast/Everglades City. The entire trip takes about seven hours with an outboard motor or nine days by canoe/kayak. Numbered markers guide you through mangrove forests, through Whitewater Bay, and around countless islands.

Campsites are available along the route. A backcountry permit is required for overnight camping. Permits may be obtained in person at the Flamingo or Gulf Coast Visitor Center no more than twenty-four hours in advance.

County: Collier and Monroe (parts of Florida Bay and Ten Thousand Islands)
Start: Flamingo marina (or Everglades City)
End: Everglades City (or Flamingo)
Distance: 99.0 miles one-way, multiday adventure, backcountry, primitive camping
Approximate float time: 7 to 10 days
Difficulty: Moderate paddling
Nearest town: Flamingo or Everglades City, depending on direction paddled
Season: Fall and winter; no later than April
Fees: Boat ramp fee or park entrance fee, depending on direction paddled
Highlights: Variety of habitats and ecosystems, mangrove tunnels
Hazards: Mosquitoes; narrow, shallow waterways
Campsites: Overnight camping, mostly primitive sites, must be prearranged with park rangers; backcountry permits required
Additional information: Bring plenty of drinking water and a compass and charts. Nautical charts are necessary for finding your way in the coastal zone and are useful in planning your trip. They may be purchased from area stores or from the Everglades Association.

Boats more than 18 feet (5.5 meters) long or with high cabins or windshields should not attempt this trip because of narrow channels and overhanging vegetation.

You may find a group or guide for this route during the winter months. Check with the park rangers, Capt. Charlie Wright, or Everglades Hostel, as well as other guide services listed in this book.

Getting there: You will need someone to pick you up at one end of the waterway and drive you back, or leave an additional vehicle at the other end for your takeout.

To begin from Everglades City, from Naples take US 41 (Tamiami Trail) east to FL 29 and head south toward Everglades City and into Everglades National Park. Launch from the boat ramp behind the park headquarters building at the Gulf Coast Ranger Station.

To begin from Homestead, the entrance to Everglades National Park is off CR 997 (Krome Avenue), which is off US 1. Go through the main gate onto FL 9336, follow the main road 38 miles to the marina at Flamingo, and launch from here.

Nine-Day Beach Trip

NOTE: This itinerary begins at the Everglades International Hostel. The Hostel is located in Homestead. From Miami, take the Florida turnpike Extension to Homestead and the Florida Keys. Stay on it until the end at Florida City Southbound and turn right at the first traffic light, SW 344 Street, (Palm Drive). Pass the next traffic

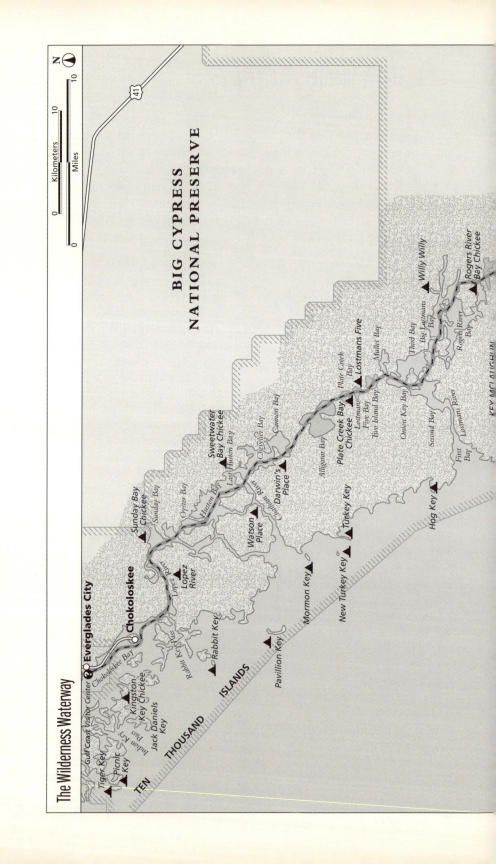

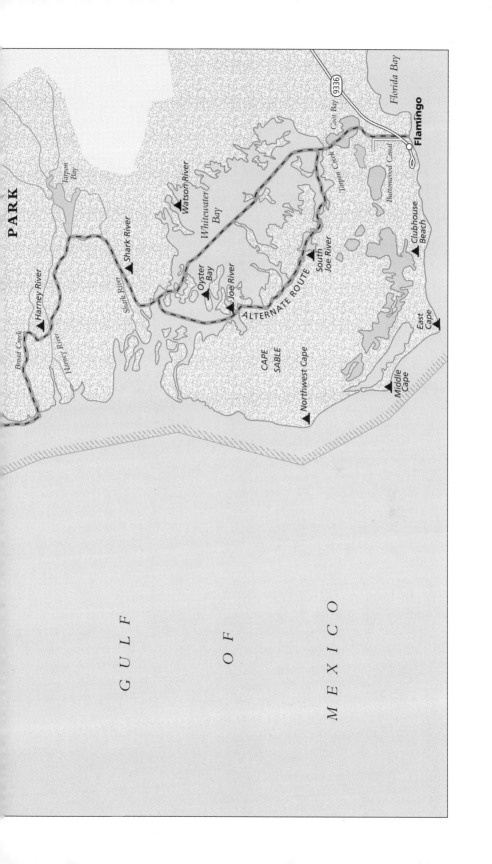

light, which is CR 997 (Krome Avenue), and make a left at Rosita's Mexican Food Restaurant onto SW 2nd Ave. The hostel is located across from the restaurant.

Day 1: Enter Turner River. Paddle through narrow mangrove tunnels and a freshwater to brackish ecosystem. Camp on Rabbit Key (saltwater ecosystem). Approximately 11.0 miles from US 41 at Turner River; 9.0 miles if leaving from Everglades City, 6.0 miles if leaving from Chokoloskee.

Day 2: Camp at Pavilion Key. Approximately 4.0 miles.

Day 3: Camp on New Turkey Key. Approximately 6.5 miles.

Day 4: Camp at Highland Beach. Approximately 11.5 miles.

Day 5: Stay at Highland Beach for a second night.

Day 6: Camp at Graveyard Creek. This ground site is sometimes very buggy. Approximately 7.0 miles.

Day 7: Camp at Oyster Bay Chickee. Approximately 10.0 miles.

Day 8: Camp on South Joe Chickee. Approximately 10.5 miles.

Day 9: Take out at Flamingo. Approximately 11.5 miles.

Five-Day Itinerary

Day 1: Begin on the Turner River, paddling through narrow tunnels in the freshwater environment. Turn east down Huddles Creek across Mud Bay and Cross Bays. Turn south at the second Cross Bay to reach the Lopez River campsite (a ground site). From Turner River at US 41 to Lopez is approximately 10.0 miles. Turner River at US 41 to Sunday Bay is approximately 13.5 miles.

Day 2: Paddle across Sunday, Oyster, Huston, and Last Huston Bays to Sweetwater Chickee (an elevated wood platform over the water). A variety of birds are often seen in this area. Approximately 11.5 miles from Lopez and 9.0 miles from Sunday Bay.

Day 3: Leave Sweetwater Chickee. Paddle south down the Chatham River and pass by the Watson Place. Camp on Mormon Key. This beach is great for sea shelling (you can bring home one quart per person). You may also find Calusa pottery on the key, but it cannot be collected. Campfires are permitted at the beach sites. Sweetwater Chickee to Mormon Key is about 7.5 miles.

Day 4: Leave Mormon Key and stop at Pavilion, which is a long white sandy beach. Paddle to Rabbit Key, another good sea-shelling area, and look for dolphins, watch shorebirds, and possibly have a campfire in the evening. This is where Ed Watson was buried after being gunned down by his neighbors. Mormon to Rabbit Key is about 8.5 miles.

Day 5: After leaving Rabbit Key stop at Jewell Key to look for mangrove tree snails. This will be your last chance to collect seashells. Return up Sandfly Pass, passing Sandfly Island, an area where people have lived in recent history. You may wish to stop here and take a hike. Following the markers in, go under the bridge and return to Everglades City. Rabbit Key to Everglades City is about 9.0 miles.

47 Sawgrass Route to Flamingo

NOTE: Special thanks to Tony Pernas of the National Park Service.

This unique paddle includes various bird species, wildlife, and even middens (shell mounds) created by Indians who camped and fished here. You will paddle through Shark River Slough and occasionally sleep in your canoe or kayak. Along the route you will encounter various ecosystems and habitats of the Everglades, including hardwood hammocks and mangrove galleys. Part of the route is along an airboat trail and will be marked. Overall, this trip should take you about three days.

County: Miami-Dade
Start: Off US 41, Canal at L-67, east of Shark Valley
End: Everglades City (or Flamingo)
Distance: 66.0 miles one-way
Approximate float time: 3 to 4 days or longer
Difficulty: Moderate to strenuous paddling, depending on water levels
Nearest town: Kendell, near Miami
Season: Best in late summer and early fall, when water will be highest
Fees: None
Highlights: Varying ecosystems, wildlife, birds, middens

Hazards: Shallow areas, saw grass, mosquitoes, alligators, and crocodiles; overnight in jungle or in canoe
Getting there: You will need someone to drop you off at the launch and then pick you up in Flamingo, or leave another vehicle at the takeout.

The launch site is off US 41, closer to the east side of the state coming from Kendell, near Miami. From Naples head east on US 41 past Everglades City and continue driving past the Oasis Visitor Center and the Shark Valley Visitor Center.

The Paddle

This unique trip gives you the opportunity to canoe the heart of the Shark River Slough. This trail starts on US 41 at the L-67 Canal. On the north side of US 41 is the monument to the crash of ValuJet Flight 592 in May 1996. The best time to take this route is when the water is at its highest, usually during late summer and early fall. Unfortunately this may also coincide with the height of mosquito season.

This trip is also distinctive in that you will be paddling through various ecosystems of the Everglades, making the transition from freshwater slough to mangrove communities. Along the way you will pass many tropical hardwood hammocks that were once inhabited by panthers.

You will see all types of birds along this route that are found in the Everglades, especially wading birds. As you paddle farther south you will see lots of middens and shell mounds. Indians—from the Calusa to the Seminoles and Miccasukee—all traveled this way, paddling their canoes or carrying them through the swamp. Don't be surprised if you see paddlers with a sail hooked up to their canoe and using the north wind to aid them as they glide through the waterways.

Day 1: For the first 10.0 miles you will be on the L-67 canal heading south. At the south end of the canal you will turn west onto a National Park Service airboat trail, marked by white PVC poles. Today the airboat trail is used primarily by law enforcement personnel and researchers. Please be careful of airboats. Although you can hear them from a distance, they may not be able to see you through the tall grass. For safety's sake, if you hear an airboat, pull off the trail.

The trail goes west for a while and eventually turns northwest. When you come to a major intersection, turn southeast on the trail, which eventually turns south-southwest. Continue paddling southwest on the trail, camping for the night around Panther Mound (sleep in boat).

Day 2: On the second day you will reach the headwaters of the Shark River, Rookery Branch. Get off the airboat trail and follow the river, which may be difficult to follow because of its many tributaries. Follow the largest tributary with the most flow. Beware of the many low-hanging branches, spiders, and other obstacles. After a while you will reach open water. Follow the river, passing Little Banana Patch on your right. Continue to Cane Patch for a well-deserved night on the ground.

Day 3: Paddle southwest, following the deeper water as it flows south. It may take you one day of paddling to reach the headwaters by the rookery. Often you can sleep in your canoe (with a backcountry permit obtained prior to your journey), or you can string a hammock across the trees in an island area or jungle hammock. This may be near the hydro stations.

Continue paddling, following the current from Rookery Branch to Shark River. From here you can paddle straight down to Flamingo or paddle along the outside of the islands and mangroves around Cape Sable. You can usually follow the airboat trails through the saw grass. This is what the rangers use when they are in the area.

You will see all types of birds along this route that you would find in the Everglades, especially wading birds.

Honorable Mentions

The Everglades Trail

The Everglades Trail is a string of twenty unique natural treasures from the headwaters of the Everglades in central Florida south to Florida Bay. You may drive from one site to the next; there is no set route. Everglades Trail signs along the highway help you navigate to each trail site, where you will find green-roofed kiosks and interpretive signs about the Everglades.

The Everglades Trail project was initiated by Wilderness Graphics, Inc., and The Nature Conservancy. Legislation creating the trail was introduced by Senator Bob Graham and created with support from Friends of Loxahatchee Refuge, the National Fish and Wildlife Foundation, the Florida Department of Environmental Protection Office of Greenways and Trails, Florida Department of Transportation, South Florida Water Management District, and Visit Florida. For more information visit www.evergladestrail.org.

If you plan on spending time at any of the points along the trail, call ahead for the best times to visit, site hours, tours, etc. This trail gives you a chance to see firsthand how the ecosystems preserve us as well. Each site offers different activities, including hiking, biking, canoeing, and boardwalks, to help visitors enjoy the wildlife and the habitat. Tram or guided boat tours are also available at some sites.

As with the other routes in this guide, it is important to be prepared. Wear sunscreen, a hat, a long-sleeved shirt, and long pants to ward off bugs as well as reflect the sun. Bring snacks and water or other fluids to stay hydrated. Binoculars, a waterproof cameras, and field guides will also increase your enjoyment.

The following is an outline of each stop along the Everglades Trail, including what the site offers and a contact number. See the map for some of the locations.

48 Shingle Creek to Lake Okeechobee

Site 1: Shingle Creek

11501 International Dr.
Orlando, FL 32821
(800) 250-4250

Activities: Hiking, biking, walking on the boardwalk, picnicking

Access: The trail for the Shingle Creek area is located behind the Marriott Resort

Shingle Creek forms the initial headwaters for the Everglades. Cypress and gum trees and wet prairies surround the area's pine islands. You can launch a canoe or kayak a few miles down the road at Hunter's Creek Middle School, on the creek's west bank. This is a good fishing area. Cast your line for panfish in the channelized 5-mile-long creek.

Site 2: The Nature Conservancy's Disney Wilderness Preserve

2700 Scrub Jay Trail
Kissimmee, FL 34759
(407) 935-0002

Activities: Interpretive exhibits, buggy tours, a boardwalk, hiking trails
Access: This preserve is southeast of Orlando. From Osceola Polk Line Road/CR 532 E, drive to South Orange Blossom Trail/US 17/US 92. Follow this 3.6 miles to South Poinciana Boulevard and turn right. Then drive 8 miles and take a slight right onto Pleasant Hill Road. Continue 0.5 miles to Old Pleasant Hill Road and then turn left. Go 0.7 miles to Scrub Jay Trail, in Kissimmee.

The preserve's 12,000 acres, located at the headwaters of the Everglades, are home to hundreds of species of wildlife.

Site 3: Lake Kissimmee State Park

14248 Camp Mack Rd.
Lake Wales, FL 33898
(863) 696-1112

Activities: Camping (primitive and RV), hiking, backpacking, horseback riding, boating. Cow Camp, a living-history site, is open on the weekends. A three-story observation tower is located north of the marina and boat launch. It is somewhat obscured by trees from the parking area. There are restrooms, picnic tables, and grills in the area under trees for groups and families.

Access: Launch from the Cow Camp weir or the boat ramp for Tiger Cove and Lake Kissimmee.

Lake Kissimmee State Park comprises 5,860 acres containing twelve plant communities, including pine flatwoods, floodplains, marshes, forests, hardwood hammocks, and backwater streams. Call the park service for updates on canoe rentals and possible ranger-led or guided tours. In the past rangers have taken paddlers out and camped overnight.

Difficulty: Easy to moderate paddling
Distance: Approximately 11.0-mile loop
Highlights: Wading birds, bald eagles, sandhill cranes, snail kites, wildlife
Hazards: Alligators, powerboats, shallow water (During drier times it may be impassible; check with ranger.)

The Paddle

Launch from Cow Camp weir into Zipprer Canal, heading west. This canal may be very shallow depending on the season and lack of rain. The canal is rather narrow and filled with vegetation for the first 1.0 mile or so. After this section you will be in a floodplain marsh, an open area. Birds you might see in this area include meadowlarks, herons, and egrets. You may also see alligators.

Lake Kissimmee State Park boat ramp. Watch out for gators; they like this area. There are lots of RVers and picnickers.

About halfway through the canal you will come to a swampy area (floodplain marsh) containing maples and sweet gum trees. In about 2.5 miles you will come out onto Lake Rosalie—a fairly shallow lake, open, with no islands.

When you come out into the lake, turn south and paddle along the shoreline. It can get windy on the open lake, making paddling a little more challenging. Staying along the shore, where there is good vegetation, will protect you from the wind.

Continue paddling in a southerly direction for 2.0 to 2.5 miles. Look for an opening to a creek, which will be wider than the canal. This is the only opening you will see that's large enough for boats to pass through. Powerboats and airboats may be your companions on this route. Rosalie Creek heads in a southeasterly direction. The only other opening along Lake Rosalie is a county boat ramp, which is south of the creek.

Rosalie Creek is a pretty, meandering creek that's also shallow. The Park Service recently cleared the creek of damage caused by a 2005 hurricane. However, you may come across some snags (downed trees) across the creek, making passage difficult. You may have to portage a little through here.

This creek zigzags back and forth, heading north, south, and east as you make your way down to Tiger Lake. The left (north) side of the creek is state park property; the right (south) side is private property. Along here you can look for globular apple snail eggs on stems of aquatic vegetation. Each mass contains twenty to thirty eggs the size of a BB. Limpkins like to feed on both the snails and the eggs. You may also see cattle grazing and wild hogs.

Continue paddling until you see the mouth of the creek going into Tiger Lake. This lake is a little deeper than Lake Rosalie. This marshy habitat is an open floodplain with some trees, roosting birds, and maybe anhingas. When you get to Tiger Lake, paddle left (northeast) along the shoreline, which is mostly floodplain marsh. About 1.0 mile along the lake is another opening, this one much wider. This is Tiger Creek, possibly two to three times wider than the Zipprer Canal. Again you may encounter boat traffic, lots of alligators, and wading birds. Tiger Creek heads north and east, with several sharp turns in the first 1.0 mile or so. Paddle northeast almost 0.5 mile before taking a sharp left, heading west. In it's 2.0 or so miles, the creek makes a half loop, heading north and then east, and then makes several more turns that head south, then north, and then east again before heading more due north to eventually dump you into Lake Kissimmee.

When you reach Lake Kissimmee, a sign at the mouth of the canal states that you are entering Lake Kissimmee State Park. Turn left and head into Tiger Cove, where you may encounter snail kites, river otters, and occasionally whooping cranes. From Tiger Cove paddle less than 1.0 mile to reach the boat dock and the marina. You will pass Cow Camp on your left, toward the southwest beyond the floodplain marsh. This large loop you just made circles Buster Island, where you can camp or hike on a 6.7-mile-long trail.

Option: If you paddle off the boat ramp into Tiger Cove and then head into Lake Kissimmee, heading east and then north, you would see lots of wading birds along

Gobbler Ridge. This is a great shorter route to explore and go birding, maybe even get some good photographs of sandhill cranes, wild turkeys, bald eagles, river otters, lots of deer, and snail kits. Snail kites, formerly called Everglades kites, feed on apple snails. They use their hook-shaped bill to get the snail out of the shell.

Bald eagles are year-round residents, with several nests in the area. They are more active during the winter months, nesting and feeding their young. It is not uncommon to see bald eagles at different stages of life here, from chicks to one-year-olds and the doting parents.

Call the park service for updates on canoe rentals and possible ranger-led or guided tours. In the past rangers have taken paddlers out and camped overnight. There is an observation tower northeast of the boat ramp that is about three stories tall. It is somewhat obscured by trees from the parking area. There are restrooms, picnic tables, and grills in the area under trees for groups and families.

Site 4: Prairie Lakes Unit, Three Lakes Wildlife Management Area

FL 523 (Canoe Creek Road)
Kenansville, FL 34474
(352) 732-1225

Activities: Hunting, fishing, hiking, camping
Access: 9 miles from Kenansville (25 miles out of St. Cloud) on FL 523 (Canoe Creek Road). These are dry prairies with birdlife.

Site 5: Kissimmee Prairie Preserve State Park

33104 Northwest 192nd Ave.
Okeechobee, FL 34972
(863) 462-5360

Activities: Camping, hiking, biking, birding, and more
Access: 7 miles from Kissimmee River

Site 6: Hickory Hammock Wildlife Management Area

US 98 between Kissimmee and Fort Basinger
(863) 462-5260; (800) 432-2045

Activities: Fishing, hiking, boating, cycling, picnicking, horseback riding, photography; wildlife viewing, including black bears and caracaras; primitive camping, equestrian campground
Access: US 98, 8 miles past the Kissimmee River Bridge and Fort Basinger

Beautiful live oaks flank the hiking trail of this 8,500-acre tract. You will also see scrub oak, hickory, and cabbage palm hammocks. This is a great birding trail. This section of the scenic trail meanders for 11.0 miles, leading north into Boney Marsh. Only 3.0 miles north, hikers will find a 25-foot-high bridge with a great view of marshes and the restored Kissimmee River. This trail heads north into Avon Park Air Force Range. However, the trail may be closed due to military endeavors. Check with park rangers before your hike. There are two nonmotorized boat launches at this site.

Site 7: Lake Okeechobee Scenic Trail (LOST)

FL 78
Okeechobee, FL
(305) 451-3005

Activities: Fishing, hiking, cycling, jogging, boating (C. Scott Driver Jr. Recreation Area); primitive camping

Access: Approximately 3 miles southwest of US 441 on FL 78

The LOST trail (110 miles of trail over Herbert Hoover Dike) has abundant wildlife, including bald eagles, snail kites, herons, egrets, wintering waterfowl, and sandhill cranes. There are primitive campsites and shelters along the way.

Lake Okeechobee is 730 square miles (451,000 acres). This shallow lake, up to 9 feet deep, is the second-largest freshwater lake in the United States and a very popular fishing hole.

Site 8: Port Mayaca Lock

18100 Southwest Conners Highway
Canal Point, FL 33438
(863) 983-8101

Activities: Hiking, fishing, wildlife photography
Access: Port Mayca Lock is on the east side of Lake Okeechobee. If you were heading south on I-95, you would want to exit onto US 91 in the Port St. Lucie area and then head west toward Indiantown and Dupuis Reserve State Forest on SW Kanner Hwy (FL 76). Follow FL 76 toward Lake Okeechobee and end at Port Mayaca, which also intersects US 441/98 or SW Conners Hwy.

Manatees, alligators and a variety of birds call the lock home.

Site 9: DuPuis Management Area

FL 76
Indiantown, FL
(561) 924-5310

Activities: Horseback riding, camping, hunting, walking along an interpretive trail; interpretive center

Access: Approximately 3 miles east of Lake Okeechobee.

This 21,875-acre multiuse natural area is on the northern edge of the original Everglades. The ecosystem here consists of ponds, wet prairies, cypress domes, pine flatwoods, and remnant Everglades marsh. Bring your binoculars and cameras to view and photograph bald eagles, herons, egrets, wood storks, and white ibis. You may also see white-tailed deer, wild hogs, and turkeys.

Site 10: Arthur R. Marshall Loxahatchee National Wildlife Refuge

10216 Lee Rd.
Boynton Beach, FL 33437
(561) 732-3684

Activities: Fishing, boating, cycling (12 miles of trails), hiking (10 miles of trails), bird watching
Access: The entrance is on US 441/FL 7, 2 miles south of the junction of FL 804 (Boynton Beach Boulevard). (In this area, US 441/FL 7 parallels I-95 and the Florida Turnpike.)
    This 147,392-acre refuge has a visitor center, butterfly garden, observation tower, fishing platform, canoe trail, and nature trails. Boat ramps are located at refuge headquarters and Hillsboro Recreation Area. Canoes are available for rental.

Difficulty: Easy to moderate paddling
Distance: 5.5-mile loop
Fees: Admission fee
Additional information: Canoe rentals are available through Loxahatchee Canoeing, Inc. (561-733-0192). The refuge hosts Everglades Day, a major annual environmental festival, in February. Call (561) 732-3684 for more information about refuge hours and programs. The refuge should not be confused with the Loxahatchee River, which is farther north.

This is a 5.5-mile loop trail within this national wildlife refuge that offers significance far beyond the enjoyment of paddling. This paddle resembles what the historic Everglades marsh would have been. It's also a great place to educate younger people on the value of what's left of the Everglades.

This paddle is through the saw grass and offers great variety. Sloughs and wet prairies (a form of marsh) encircle tree islands dominated by coastal plains willow, with coco plum and wax myrtle. Wildflowers offer a pageantry and primrose willow and dahoon holly can be found among the trees and shrubs. Ferns grow in untamed profusion. Whatever season you visit, the plants are a palette of colors.

This refuge is known for its birding with more than 200 species of birdlife. More common are great blue herons, tricolor herons, ibis, and great egrets. Snail kites (Everglade kites) nest in the refuge. Wood storks, limpkins, and glossy ibis can be observed in a natural habitat.

Other wildlife can be seen while you are paddling or even walking on the boardwalk. Deer can be seen in open vistas. There is a heavy alligator population. Bass are also plentiful.

The Paddle

The Arthur R. Marshall Loxahatchee National Wildlife Refuge is named for Art Marshall, a passionate defender of wilderness and wild things. The staff and volunteers are equally passionate about their wild place.

A paddling trail has been carved by machine through the saw grass, and volunteers and dedicated staff keep the trail open. There are interpretive signs at several locations along the trail.

At about the midway point, there is a floating dock with a platform. Mile markers and directional arrows keep the paddler informed and on the trail. Paddling off the trail is not a good idea, since the way is often hard to find in a vast landscape of visually similar tree islands.

When the water level is right, guided tours sometimes depart from the loop to cross an area of wet prairie. A wet prairie is a peat-bottomed marsh that is flooded 50 to 150 days a year. Because of the flooding interval, wet prairies are rich in grasses, sedges, and flowers.

Perhaps the best way to experience this trail is to savor it. Somewhere between Mile 2 and 3, stop paddling, close your eyes and feel the sun beating down while the wildlife around the boat begins to ignore you and goes about the business of living. Experience how the Everglades feels and sounds. This is indeed the Everglades as close to the original as we are likely to come.

Additional paddling is possible on L-40, a canal that travels more than 50 miles through the refuge. While wide and boated, the canal offers additional wildlife viewing. It is too long, however, for a single day's paddle and there is no camping along the trail.

There are plans to expand the current trail with a second loop and perhaps add overnight camping options. The trail may be closed during low water, so check before you visit.

Sunblock, water, and a hat are good precautions. There is a short deerfly season, but in summer this area lacks the infamous saltwater mosquitoes found in Everglades National Park. It still has a few pesky natives though.

Great blue heron. Arthur R. Marshall Loxahatchee Refuge is chock-full of beautiful birds as well as flora and fauna. ▶

Great egret foraging for food. More than 200 species of birds can be found at Loxahatchee Refuge.

Site 11: Everglades Wildlife Management Area

Alligator Alley Rest Area, I-75 at Mile Marker 36
(954) 746-1789

The rest area has restrooms, a boat ramp, wildlife exhibits, wading birds, and an observation platform. Bring your camera.

Site 12: Biscayne National Park

9700 Southwest 328th St.
Homestead, FL 33033
(305) 230-PARK

Activities: Glass-bottom boat tours, canoeing, kayaking, sailing, snorkeling, scuba diving
Access: From the Florida Turnpike: Take the Turnpike south to exit 6 (Speedway Boulevard). Turn left from the exit ramp and continue south to SW 328th Street (North Canal Drive). Turn left and continue to the end of the road. It is approximately 5 miles and the entrance will be on your left. From US 1: Drive south to Homestead. Turn left on SW 328th Street

Roseate Spoonbills. Beautiful year-round residents. You will see many of these, especially around the Ten Thousand Islands.

(North Canal Drive) and continue to the end of the road. It is approximately nine miles and the entrance will be on your left.
Additional information: For information on glass-bottom boat tours, snorkeling, scuba diving, kayak and canoe rentals, and picnic areas, call (305) 230-1100.

Unlike other parks, which are predominantly on land, Biscayne National Park is for paddlers and boaters—a treasure of water and blue skies. Paddlers who snorkel can enjoy the coral reefs and colorful, exotic tropical fish. This is also a haven for divers and fishermen.

The Paddle

Glide through the mangrove shoreline—a labyrinth of roots that provide a nursery for fish. Branches and treetops create a rookery for beautiful birds like white ibis, blue herons, and snowy egrets. These colonies of birds forage for prey in the shallow waters. Species of fauna and flora from Florida to the West Indies can be seen here, such as gumbo-limbo trees, Jamaican dogwood, strangler fig, devil's potato, satin-leaf touchwood, and mahogany. In these hardwood hammocks you will also see butterflies, including the rare Schaus swallowtail.

Be sure to keep a compass and weatherproof chart handy while navigating through this floating jungle.

Site 13: Everglades National Park, Ernest F. Coe Visitor Center

40001 FL 9336
Homestead, FL 33034
(305) 242-7700

The visitor center contains an interpretive center, a gift shop, and restrooms.

Site: 14: Everglades National Park, Shark Valley Area

Off US 41 (Tamiami Trail)
(305) 221-8776

Activities: Bike (rentals available), hike, or take the tram to the observation tower.
Access: Shark Valley Visitor Center is located on US 41 (Tamiami Trail) 25 miles west of the Florida Turnpike, exit 25A (from the north) and exit 25 (from the south). From Naples, take US 41 approximately 70 miles east to Shark Valley.

The Everglades offers a variety of interesting ecosystems, including sawgrass marshes, prairies, and hardwood hammocks.

Site: 15: Big Cypress National Preserve

33100 Tamiami Trail East
Ochopee, FL 34141
(239) 695-1201

Activities: Scenic drives, bird watching, swamp walks, canoeing, and biking on own or on ranger led trip
Access: Big Cypress National Preserve is located in southwest Florida between Miami and Naples. I-75 (Alligator Alley) and US 41 (Tamiami Trail) are the main roads that traverse the site. Preserve headquarters is located near Naples, along US 41, 5 miles east of FL 29 intersection.

Park information, a short film, and exhibits are available at the Big Cypress Visitor Center.

Site 16: Everglades National Park, Gulf Coast Visitor Center

Everglades City, FL
(239) 695-3311

Activities: Boat tours, canoeing, kayaking
Access: The Gulf Coast Visitor Center is located 5 miles south of US 41 (Tamiami Trail) on FL 29 in Everglades City. From I-75 (Alligator Alley), take exit 80 (FL29) south and proceed 20 miles to Everglades City. Follow the signs to the visitor center; it will be on your right.

The visitor center has park information, snacks, a gift shop with guidebooks and field guides, restrooms, and a boat ramp.

Site 17: Fakahatchee Strand Preserve State Park

137 Coastline Dr.
Copeland, FL 34137
(239) 695-4593

Activities: Hiking, boardwalk, swamp walks
Access: Fakahatchee Strand Preserve State Park is located on Janes Memorial Scenic Drive, just west of Copeland on FL 29. It is several miles north of the intersection of FL 29 and US 41.

The park contains a self-guided boardwalk and 60 miles of hiking trails. Park staff offers guided swamp walks during winter months.

Site 18: Collier-Seminole State Park

20200 East Tamiami Trail
Naples, FL 34114
(239) 394-3397

Activities: Hiking, camping, biking, birding (best in fall and winter) in mangroves and hardwood hammocks. Also enjoy paddle routes in Everglades City/Gulf Coast section.
Access: The entrance to Collier-Seminole State Park is off US 41 (Tamiami Trail). Collier-Seminole State Park is 17 miles south of Naples. Heading south from Tampa on I-75, take exit 101 (FL 951 and FL 84) and turn right. Turn left on US 41 and then Collier-Seminole State Park will be 8 miles on the right just past CR 92. Coming west from Ft. Lauderdale, take exit 80 (FL 29), go south to US 41 and turn right. Follow US 41 for about 15 miles and Collier-Seminole State Park will be on your left. The ramp is inside the park; follow signs to boat launch, about 0.5 mile in. Register at the ranger station: (239) 642-8898 or (239) 394-3397.

Site 19: Rookery Bay National Estuarine Research Reserve

300 Tower Rd.
Naples, FL 34113
(239) 417-6310

Activities: Wildlife observation, exploration
Access: Take I-75 south to old exit 15 (new exit 101), and bear right onto Collier Boulevard, CR 951 (heading toward Marco Island). Follow this road for approximately 5-7 miles across the intersection at US 41 south. Go another 1 mile and Comcast will be on your right. That is Tower Road. Make a right onto Tower Road and turn left into the parking lot.

Here you can observe wildlife, explore various habitats, and learn about estuaries. There's a visitor center and gift shop.

Site 20: Florida Panther National Wildlife Refuge

3860 Tollgate Blvd., Suite 300
Naples, FL 34114
(239) 353-8442

Activities: Walking
Access: From Naples, take I-75 south towards Miami, exit 80. Turn left on FL 29 heading north. The refuge trails will be on the left side of the road about 0.5 mile down. The refuge contains a walking trail through Florida panther habitat.

Appendix A: Resources

Paddlers Checklist

__ Personal floatation device (PFD), one per person
__ Paddles, preferably with one spare
__ Bailer
__ Bow and stern lines
__ Dry bags, waterproof bags for gear (cameras, etc.)
__ Lights, flashlights, extra batteries (if going out at night)
__ Waterproof charts, or a large enough bag to carry nautical charts in
__ Compass, and maybe a spare
__ Tide chart
__ Binoculars
__ Backcountry permit
__ Fishing license and regulations, if you will be fishing
__ Weather forecast
__ Tent, netting (for protection against mosquitoes and no-see-ums)
__ Sleeping bag and pad, or a space blanket
__ Drinking water, one gallon per person per day
__ Food, with extra supply
__ Animal-proof container for food and/or water
__ Portable stove or grill (for trips when cooking out or camping overnight)
__ Fuel for stove
__ Waterproof matches, lighter
__ Cooking gear and utensils
__ Rain gear
__ Biodegradable soap
__ Cold- and warm-weather clothing
__ Long-sleeve pants and shirt for sun protection
__ Hat
__ First-aid kit
__ Knife
__ Watch
__ Sunglasses
__ Sunscreen and lip balm
__ Insect repellent
__ Transistor or weather radio
__ Personal items; toothbrush, etc.
__ Trowel

__ Biodegradable toilet paper
__ Flare(s)
__ Emergency whistle, should be on your PFD
__ Field guides for birds, reptiles, plants, etc., of South Florida
__Cell phone with extra battery

Government Agencies

The following agencies can provide additional information on the Everglades and surrounding area.

Big Cypress National Preserve, Ochopee Visitor Center

(239) 695-1201 or (239) 695-4111
www.nps.gov/bicy

Collier-Seminole State Park

20200 East Tamiami Trail
Naples, FL 34114
(239) 394-3397
www.dep.state.fl.us/parks/district4/collier-seminole
The state park offers overnight camping (RV and primitive), a boat launch, and hiking and biking trails. For camping reservations call Reserve America at (800) 326-3521.

Everglades National Park, Gulf Coast Visitor Center

(239) 695-3311
www.nps.gov/ever
Everglades City is located near Chokoloskee Bay. The visitor center offers guided tours, talks, and bike rides. Call or visit the park's Web site for a schedule of events. You can launch from the ramp at the visitor center; from the boat ramp at City Seafood, just up the road; or farther south at Chokoloskee Causeway.

A twelve-month Everglades National Park pass is available for $25. An annual national park pass ($50) allows admission to any national park.

Bicycles can be rented year-round at both the Flamingo marina and Shark Valley Visitor Plaza. Skiffs, canoes, and kayaks are also available for rent by calling (239) 695-3101.

Guided hikes, canoe tours, and swamp tromps are offered by park rangers. Most are offered year round but are limited during the summer months.

Two-hour guided tram tours (Shark Valley Tram Tours; 305-221-8455) take you on a journey through saw grass prairie and small tree islands. Your guide will identify various trees, plants, birds, alligators, and other flora and fauna. The tram stops at an observation tower.

Additional Useful Phone Numbers

Park headquarters and information: (305) 242-7700
Campground reservations: (800) 365-2267
Emergencies: (305) 242-7740 or #NPS (cell phone)
Everglades City Boat Tours: (239) 695-2591 or (800) 445-7724
Flamingo Boat Tours/Rentals: (239) 695-3101

Fakahatchee Strand State Preserve

137 Coast Line Dr.
P.O. Box 548
Copeland, FL 33926
(239) 695-4593
www.floridastateparks.org/fakahatcheestrand

Ten Thousand Islands National Wildlife Refuge

3860 Tollgate Blvd., Suite 300
Naples, FL 34114
(239) 353-8442
www.fws.gov/southeast/TenThousandIsland/

Rookery Bay National Estuarine Research Reserve

300 Tower Rd.
Naples, FL 34113
(239) 417-6310
www.rookerybay.org

Florida Department of Environmental Protection District Offices

South District (west side of Everglades)
2295 Vistoria Ave., Suite 364
Fort Myers, FL 33902-2549
(941) 332-6975
www.dep.state.fl.us/water/wetlands

Southeast District (east side of Everglades, Flamingo to Homestead)
400 North Congress Ave.
West Palm Beach, FL 33416
(561) 681-6600
www.dep.state.fl.us/water/wetlands

Water Management Districts

South Florida
3301 Gun Club Rd.
West Palm Beach, FL 33406
(561) 686-8800
www.sfwmd.gov

Florida Fish and Wildlife Conservation Commission

www.myfwc.com

Everglades City Chamber of Commerce

P.O. Box 130
Everglades City, FL 33929
(239) 695-3941 or (800) 226-9609
www.florida-everglades.com

Tropical Everglades Visitor Association

(Information on Flamingo, Florida City, and Homestead)
160 US Highway 1
Florida City, FL 33034
(800) 388-9669

Homestead & Florida City Chamber of Commerce

212 NW 1st Ave., Homestead, FL 33030
(305) 247-2332

Guides, Tours, and Rentals

Guide Services

Capt. Charlie Wright
Everglades Area Tours
P.O. Box 670
Everglades City, FL 34139
(239) 695-9107
www.evergladesareatours.com
Ten Thousand Islands fishing guide, ecotours, day trips and multiple-day adventures, birding and photography, outfit rentals

Canoe/Kayak Rentals

North American Canoe Tours (at the Ivey House)
107 Camellia St.
P.O. Box 5038
Everglades City, FL 34139
(239) 695-3299
www.evergladesadventures.com

Everglades Area Tours

Captain Charlie Wright
P.O. Box 670
Everglades City, FL 34139
(239) 695-9107
www.evergladesareatours.com

Everglades City Airboat and Ecotours

Billie Swamp Safari: (863) 983-6101 or (800) 949-6101, Big Cypress Seminole Indian Reservation, between Fort Lauderdale and Naples off of I-75 (at exit 49) and then north for 19 miles.

Captain Bob's Excellent Adventure and Everglades Day Safari: (239) 437-2095 or (888) 847-9074. They can pick you up in one of five locations, complete with airboat and conventional boat tours, lunch, wildlife drive, and nature walk.

Captain Doug's Everglades Tours: (800) 282-9194, 1.0 mile past the bridge on FL 29 in Everglades City.

Everglades Private Airboat Tours: (239) 695-4637, 23 miles east of Naples on 41, 1 mile before FL 29.

Jungle Erv's: (800) 432-3367 Ticket headquarters is located on US 41, 0.5 mile west of FL 29 and visitor center.

Speedy Johnsons: (239) 695-4448, follow US 41 to FL 29 into Everglades City. Take the first right after the bridge and go 1 block onto Begonia Street.

Totch's Island Tours: (239) 695-2333, 929 Dupont Street, take US 41 35 miles from Naples, south on FL 29, and then go 3 miles to Dupont Street.

Wooten's: (800) 282-2781, 32330 Tamiami Trail East, Ochopee, 1.5 miles east on US 41 from FL 29.

Air Tours

Wings Ten Thousand Islands Areo Tours (at the Everglades Airport)
650 Everglade City Airpark Rd.
Box 244
Chokoloskee, FL, 34238
(239) 695-3296
Flight tours over the Keys, the Dry Tortugas, the Everglades, or the Ten Thousand Islands in an Alaskan floatplane.

Fishing

Fishing licenses are available by calling (888) FISH-FLORIDA or in person at area Walmarts and the Everglades City Library (102 Copeland Ave. North; 239-695-2511).

Everglades City Tackle Shops

Glades Haven: (239) 695-2214
Win-Car Hardware: (239) 695-3201
Outdoor Resorts Marina: (239) 695-2881

Appendix B: Attractions

Museums

The Museum of the Everglades

105 West Broadway
Everglades City, FL 34139
(239) 695-0008
Open Tuesday through Friday 9:00 a.m. to 5:00 p.m., Saturday 9:00 a.m. to 4:00 p.m. Located off Broadway Street, the museum building used to be a commercial laundry facility for the Collier Corporation. The museum hosts art displays, which change almost monthly. They occasionally offer guided walking tours of historic buildings and other events.

The Smallwoods Store and Museum, a historic landmark on Chokoloskee Island. Open for visitors.

The Smallwoods Store and Museum

P.O. Box 367,
Chokoloskee, FL 33925
(239) 695-2989
Open daily 10:00 a.m. to 5:00 p.m.
Small fee
This is the site of a historic store that used to trade with the Indians and was the site of the 1910 gang killing of Edgar Watson. In 1982 the building was restored as a museum highlighting Florida pioneer history. Located at the end of Chokoloskee Island.

Other Attractions

Everglades Spa and Lodge

201 Broadway West
Everglades City, FL 34139
(239) 695-1066 or (239) 695-3151
Located in the historic Bank of the Everglades building, the only bank in Collier County for almost twenty-six years. Facing the river in the heart of the city, the spa attracts clients by boat and by car. They offer skin care, body wraps, acupuncture, intense light therapy, and colon hydrotherapy.

Big Cypress National Preserve

(239) 695-4111
www.nps.gov/bicy
The Oasis Visitor Center is located off US 41, about 20 miles from Everglades City. There is a small boardwalk in front of the building along a small body of water that hosts alligators. The Florida Scenic Trail, a trail system that spans the state of Florida, passes directly through Big Cypress. Loop Road—a 23-mile, one-lane dirt road—begins at Monroe Station and ending near Shark Valley. This road passes through a beautiful cypress forest that's often filled with feeding ibis and sunning alligators.

H. P. Williams Wayside

Turner River Road: Located on US 41 about 7 miles east of Everglades City. A small interpretive boardwalk overlooks the Turner River Canal. Alligators and a variety birds can bee seen swimming and feeding here. You can drive the dirt road to expand your wildlife viewing. By connecting Turner River and Birdon Roads you can create a 17-mile, U-shape drive through predominantly open-grass prairie dotted with slash pine and bald cypress.

Kirby Storter

Located on FL 41, 13 miles east of Everglades City is a 1.0-mile boardwalk into the cypress forest.

Fire Prairie Trail

This 5.0-mile, round-trip, hiking, natural trail begins 14 miles north of US 41, off Turner River Road. The trail follows an old oil road through a hardwood and cypress forest and across an open prairie to an old oil pad.

Fakahatchee Strand State Preserve

Headquarters: 137 Coast Line Dr.
Copeland, FL 34137
(239) 695-4593
www.floridastateparks.org/fakahatcheestrand
This is the world's only bald cypress–royal palm forest. The Fakahatchee Strand provides valuable habitat for tropical plants because the large size of the swamp and its deep sloughs create a humid, frost-free environment in an otherwise subtropical area. More native orchid species grow in this 75,000-acre wilderness than any other place on the continent. The preserve's headquarters are located in Copeland, 5 miles north of Everglades City off FL 29. Ranger-led activities can include swamp walks and orchid talks.

Big Cypress Bend Boardwalk

Located 7 miles from Everglades City on US 41 (Tamiami Trail), this 2,000-foot boardwalk extends into an old-growth bald cypress swamp with 500- to 600-year-old bald cypress trees. At the end of the boardwalk is a beautiful alligator hole populated by a variety of wading and diving birds, as well as one or two adult alligators with a few generations of immature alligators. Often seen here are red-shouldered hawks, bald eagles, several different species of snakes, raccoons, barred owls, turtles, and anoles. A Native American gift store near the trailhead offers handmade gifts and souvenirs.

Rookery Bay National Estuarine Research Reserve

300 Tower Rd.
Naples, FL 34113
(239) 417-6310
www.rookerybay.org/
Located at the north end of Ten Thousand Islands, off FL 951 toward Marco Island, the reserve is one of the few remaining undisturbed mangrove estuaries in North America. The preserve contains an educational learning center offering such interest-

ing programs as Shark Facts, Skulls & Bones, and Munchin in the Mangroves. An art gallery showcases traveling art displays.

There are several walking trails nearby, along Shell Island Road, with botanical signage. Shell Point Canoe Trail is marked and takes you through mangrove tunnels, mudflats, oyster beds, and rookery islands. The Briggs Boardwalk is a 0.5-mile loop through rare coastal scrub, pine flatwoods, and marsh habitat. Primitive camping is permitted in designated areas.

Rod & Gun Club

200 Riverside Dr.
Everglades City, FL 34139
(239) 695-2101
Built in late 1800s, the Rod & Gun Club has dark interior woodwork with animal trophies on display. Dining is available inside and out. A screened porch faces the Barron River. This is also a hotel.

Lodging and Dining

Ivey House Bed and Breakfast and Guest Inn

107 Camellia St.
P.O. Box 5038
Everglades City, FL 34139
(239) 695-3299
www.iveyhouse.com
The Ivey House offers canoe and kayak rentals (guests save 20 percent) and guided tours

Barron River Motel, Marina, and RV Park

P.O. Box 116
Everglades City, FL 32139
(239) 695-3331 or (800) 535-4961
www.evergladespark.com

Everglades City Motel

310 Collier Ave.
Everglades City, FL 34139
(239) 695-4224 or (800) 695-8353
www.evergladescitymotel.com

On the Banks of the Everglades B&B Inn

201 West Broadway
P.O. Box 570
Everglades City, FL 34139
(239) 695-3151 or (888) 431-1977
http://www.inntravels.com/usa/fl/everglades.html

Outdoor Resorts

Outdoor Resorts Chokoloskee
P.O. Box 429
Chokoloskee Island, FL 34138
(239) 695-3788 or (239) 695-2881
Offers an RV park, motel, marina, and canoe ramp.

Everglades International Hostel

20 Southwest Second Ave.
Florida City, FL 33034
(800) 372-3874
www.evergladeshostel.com
Guided tours and canoe rentals.

Rod & Gun Club

200 Riverside Dr.
Everglades City, FL 34139
(239) 695-2101
Accommodations and dining in a late 1800s building with a hunting motif.

Appendix C: Animals of the Everglades

Birds

Everglades National Park boasts more than 350 species of birds. The following list identifies them by groups (L=length, WS=wingspan).

Shorebirds

Sanderling—Small, white; gregarious; chases waves on the beach (8" L, 17" WS).
Black-bellied Plover—Winter plumage drab gray; sports black belly before migrating (11.5" L, 29" WS).
Ruddy Turnstone—Very short legs; uses wedge-shaped bill to turn over shells to search for prey (9.5" L, 21" WS).
Spotted Sandpiper—Found in winter without spot on its underside; tail bobs as bird forages along the edge of mudflats (8" L, 15" WS).
Greater Yellowlegs—Slender, with long, distinctly yellow legs; call: a loud "whew" (14" L, 28" WS).

Tri-colored heron foraging for food.

Dunlin—Seen in flocks; last of shorebirds to return to south Florida in the fall (8" L, 17" WS).
Lesser Yellowlegs—Feeds in groups in both fresh- and saltwater ponds; call: a two-syllable "too-too" (10.5" L, 24" WS).
Short-billed Dowitcher—Probes with sewing machine–like motion; prefers saltwater habitats (11" L, 19" WS).
Semi-palmated Plover—Short, stubby bill to pluck marine worms from mudflats (7" L, 19" WS).
Wilson's Plover—Heavy bill, long for a plover, separates it from the other small plovers (7.5" L, 19" WS).
Piping Plover—Short stubby bill and orange legs; declining in population (7" L, 19" WS).
Willet—Gray bird in winter plumage; striking white wing pattern in flight (15" L, 26" WS).
Killdeer—Shorebird that's often found far from water; common throughout United States; only plover with a double-ring collar (10" L, 24" WS).
Black-necked Stilt—Only shorebird with long pink legs; has a sharp incessant call (14" L, 29" WS).

Wading Birds

There are sixteen different species of wading birds in the Everglades; a few are listed below. These birds have long legs for wading into the water to catch their food.

White ibis—the most common wading bird in the Everglades; prefers crayfish and has a long, slender, curved beak it uses for probing the mud for food. Ancient Egyptians believed the Sacred Ibis to be the reincarnation of their God Thoth, the god of wisdom and learning (25" L, 38" WS).

Great Blue Heron—Solitary, stately; stalks its prey. The white form, often confused with the Great Egret, is found mostly in south Florida (48" L, 72" WS).

Wood Stork—An excellent messenger of the past, present, and future. Like the wood stork, the Everglades ecosystem is endangered. A pair of endangered wood storks need about 440 pounds of fish during a breeding season to feed themselves and their young. They like to nest in colonies in treetops and swamps (40" L, 61" WS).

Mammals

The following mammals are known residents of the Everglades:

Atlantic bottlenose dolphin	Raccoon
Black bear	River otter
Bobcat	West Indian manatee
Everglades mink	White-tailed deer
Florida panther	

Bottlenose Dolphin

Bottlenose dolphins can hold their breath up to twenty minutes, and some have been tracked more than 0.5 mile below the surface. Dolphins can swim at speeds of 20 miles per hour and can live to be forty years old. Dolphins get all the water they need from the food they eat. When dolphins poke their head above water to look around, it is called spy hopping. When they leap from the water and fall back with a big splash, it is called breaching.

Dolphins probably do not sleep. Part of their brain is always alert because they must surface to breathe. Each bottlenose dolphins makes a signature whistle made up of a unique pattern of sounds. They are used like a dolphin's name to identify it among all the others.

You can tell a dolphin's age by its teeth. The teeth grow in layers, year by year. The rings in a tooth's cross-section can be counted like rings on a tree stump.

Dolphins have hand and finger bones inside their flippers, which are similar to human arms. Their fins and the flukes have no bones at all.

Manatees

Zoologists can determine the age of a manatee by counting the number of growth rings on its ear bone. Each ring equals one year. Although zoologists are not sure of manatees' longevity, they may live as long as sixty years.

Most mammals have seven neck bones; manatees have only has six. Because of this they are not able to turn their heads to see—they have to move their whole body. They require water temps of 68 degrees Fahrenheit or warmer.

Manatees are farsighted and can see up to 130 feet. It takes nearly seven days for a manatee to digest one meal. An adult manatee may eat up to one hundred pounds of water plants per day and may spend up to eight hours a day just feeding. After every meal they clean their teeth, removing the grass and dirt caught between their teeth by rolling small rocks around inside their mouths.

Manatees can stay underwater for up to twenty minutes; however, they usually surface to breathe every three to five minutes. They even float up for air in the middle of a nap and then sink back down to continue sleeping. Manatees don't usually dive more than 10 feet; however, they can dive as deep as 33 feet.

Manatees travel at about 2 to 6 miles per hour but can achieve speeds of 15 miles per hour. A newborn weighs at least sixty pounds and is about 4 feet long.

Areas frequented by manatees have been posted. Keep an eye out for these aquatic mammals. If you're in a powerboat, slow to an idle if you observe manatees, but do not approach or molest them.

Reptiles

Everglades reptiles include the American alligator, the American crocodile and various turtles, snakes, and lizards.

Alligators prefer freshwater, while crocodiles can better tolerate seawater due to specialized glands for filtering out salt. However both can survive in either. Alligators have wider and shorter heads and a more U-shaped than V-shaped snout. The alligator's upper jaw is wider than its lower jaw and the teeth in the lower jaw fit into small depressions in the upper jaw. The upper and lower jaws of the crocodiles are the same width and teeth in the lower jaw fall along the edge or outside of the upper jaw when the mouth is closed. The alligator also tends to be darker in color than crocs. It is reported that crocodiles are almost invariably more aggressive in their natural habitat.

Alligators

An alligator is a crocodilian in the genus Alligator of the family Alligatoridae, (scientific classification: Class: Reptilia).

Eggs incubated between 90 and 93 degrees Fahrenheit produce males; temperatures between 82 and 86 degrees produce females. Newborns are 8 to 9 inches long and grow about 1 foot per year until the age of six. Young gators remain with their mother for two to three years.

Alligators see in color. At night male alligators' eyes appear red; females' appear yellow. Their heart beats as slow as five beats per minute in cool water (50 degrees Fahrenheit) and as quick as forty-five beats per minute in warm water (82 degrees). Alligators store fat in their body and can survive as long as one or two years without eating.

Gators have been observed running on land as fast as 26 miles per hour. They can hold their breath underwater for up to six hours. Adult alligators can eat as much as 20 percent of their total body weight in one meal. The alligator cannot move its tongue and must raise his head in order to swallow its food.

Turtles

Common turtles found in the park include the striped mud turtle, along the Anhinga Trail; the peninsula cooter, seen in Shark Valley; and the Florida red-belly, found in freshwater marshes and ponds.

In the pinelands or a hammock, you might encounter a Florida box turtle. Another Everglades land turtle is the gopher tortoise, found in the southwestern area called Cape Sable. Here you might also see a diamondback terrapin along the shoreline. This species likes the brackish water of the mangrove estuary. The loggerhead turtle, which nests at night during the summer months along Highland Beach at Cape Sable and Sandy Key in Florida Bay, is a nationally threatened species.

Many turtles have been displaced when their nesting environments are invaded by development.

Snakes

Snakes can be found everywhere in the Everglades. They range in size from the poisonous dusky pygmy rattlesnake, seldom more than 2 feet long, to the eastern indigo snake (up to 8 feet long). There are twenty-seven species of snakes in Everglades National Park. Only four are venomous: the Florida cottonmouth or water moccasin, diamondback rattlesnake, dusky pygmy rattlesnake, and coral snake.

The most common snake in the Everglades is the brown water snake, which is often seen along the Anhinga Trail. It is often mistaken for the venomous Florida cottonmouth. The brown water snake will bite if cornered or mistreated; however, it is not poisonous.

Most snakes adapt to freshwater environments, although some, like the cottonmouth and mangrove salt marsh snake, can survive in mangrove swamps and saltwater marshes. Some snakes in the park are beautifully colored; others are drab to blend in with their environment. The highly venomous eastern coral snake (red, yellow, and black rings and a black snout) uses its bright colors to warn predators. This snake can be found in hardwood hammocks and pinelands under leaves, rocks, and logs. The Florida scarlet snake and scarlet kingsnake imitate the coral snake in appearance and are found in the same habitat. All three species have red, black, and yellow rings, but the Florida scarlet and scarlet kingsnake have red snouts. In the coral snake, the red and yellow rings touch. The Florida scarlet snake and scarlet kingsnake have their red and yellow rings separated by black.

The striped crayfish snake, considered the best-swimming snake in Florida, can only be found among the marsh plants in the northern part of the park.

Another group of snakes found in the park are the rat snakes. The Everglades rat snake is a bright orange with four dark stripes; the corn snake has reddish blotches with a black border in the background of gray, tan, yellow, or orange; and the yellow rat snake has four black stripes on a bright golden-yellow background. The body of the Everglades rat snake is shaped like a loaf of bread, not round like most snakes. Good climbers, they feed on birds' eggs, small rodents, frogs, and toads.

Lizards

The tiny green anole makes a lot of noise in the hammocks. A brown blur, it scurries up fig trees and out onto the leaves. The lizard transforms into a sliver of green, camouflaging itself in the foliage. The male anole is noticeable when his bright-red throat pouch protrudes. They do this to attract a mate and to alert others of territorial ownership.

The lizard's beacon is easily visible from many trees away. Female anoles scamper to check out the male lizard, while another hammock resident approaches. Soon the green anole, once a star performer in this tiny verdant arena, is a snack for a corn snake.

The native green anole, once very common throughout the park is being replaced in the pineland and hammocks by the exotic brown anole, native of Cuba.

The Florida reef gecko is the state's only native gecko. It resides in the hammocks and pinelands under rocks and leaves and is the smallest lizard in North America (2 to 2.25 inches).

The glass lizard is common in freshwater marshes and flooded pinelands. Glass lizards can be seen along the road during high water or after a fire in their habitat. They may be up to 2 feet long.

Exotic lizards also adapt to the Everglades, where they compete for food, shelter, and territory. Many of these exotics are former pets that have escaped or have been released into the park.

Amphibians

Including frogs, toads, and salamanders, amphibians spend the first part of their life in water, breathing through gills. As adults, they may still live in water but use lungs to breathe. You will probably hear them and not see them, as amphibians are mostly nocturnal and very well camouflaged.

Frogs: The little grass frog is the tiniest frog in North America. If you spot one, you may think it's a baby frog. Grass frogs can be found near water clinging to saw grass. You can hear their breeding song at night.

The pig frog's gruntlike call can be heard day or night, year-round. They can be found on the Anhinga Trail and in Shark Valley, in the park's freshwater marshes.

Toads: At the main visitor center during summer, you may be greeted by a chorus of oak toads. They are found in hammocks, pinelands, and wet saw grass.

Salamanders: The Everglades dwarf siren is a salamander found only in the Everglades.

Threatened and Endangered Species

The following species are either threatened or endangered:

American crocodile
Green turtle
Atlantic Ridley turtle
Atlantic hawksbill turtle
Atlantic leatherback turtle
Cape Sable seaside sparrow
Snail (Everglades) kite
Wood stork

West Indian manatee
Florida panther
Key Largo wood rat
Key Largo cotton mouse
Red-cockaded woodpecker
Schaus swallowtail butterfly
Garber's spurge (plant)

Appendix D: Fishing in the Everglades

There are more than 300 species of fish in the Everglades.

One-third of Everglades National Park is covered by water, creating excellent boating and fishing opportunities. Snapper, sea trout, redfish, bass, and bluegill are plentiful. Saltwater fishing sites include Florida Bay, Ten Thousand Islands, and elsewhere in the park's coastal zone. Freshwater and saltwater fishing require separate Florida fishing licenses.

Fishing from the shore is very limited. However, park waters provide thousands of acres of shallow-water flats, channels, and mangrove keys in which to fish. Before leaving shore, think safety! Be aware of local boating conditions, especially weather and tides.

Fishing Regulations: Freshwater and Saltwater

General

- All waters from, and including, Nine Mile Pond northward along the main park road are considered freshwater.

- Anglers may have four fillets per person for immediate consumption at designated campsites or on board vessels equipped with cooking facilities. All other fish must remain whole while on park waters.

Commercial Fishing

- All commercial fishing is prohibited in Everglades National Park.

Prohibited Fishing Gear

- Except for dip nets, cast nets, and landing nets, all other seines and nets are prohibited.

- The use and possession of spear guns and spear poles are prohibited.

Freshwater License

- A Florida freshwater fishing license is required to fish in freshwater or to possess freshwater species.

Bait

- Live or dead fish (including minnows and shiners) or amphibians, and nonpreserved fish eggs or roe, are prohibited.

- Digging for bait inside the park is not permitted.

Areas Closed to Fishing

- No fishing is allowed at the Ernest F. Coe (Main) Visitor Center lakes; Royal Palm Visitor Center area and trails; Chekika Lake; along the first 3 miles of the main park road, including Taylor Slough; or along the Shark Valley Tram Road.

Mercury Warning!

- High levels of mercury have been found in Everglades bass and in some fish species in northern Florida Bay.

- Do not eat bass caught north of the main park road.

- Do not eat bass caught south of the main park road more than once a week.

- Children and pregnant women should not eat any bass from these waters.

- The following saltwater species caught in northern Florida Bay should not be consumed more than once per week by adults or once per month by children and women of child-bearing age: spotted sea trout, gafftopsail catfish, bluefish, crevalle jack, or ladyfish.

Saltwater License

- A Florida saltwater fishing license is required to fish in salt water or to possess saltwater species.

Bait

- Saltwater bait includes shrimp, minnows, pilchards, pinfish, mullet, mojarras (shad), and ballyhoo.

- Bait, except for mullet and shrimp, is not included in bag limits.

- Bait may be taken with hook and line, dip net (not wider than 3 feet/0.9 meter), and cast net.

Areas Closed to Fishing

- No fishing is allowed in Eco, Mrazek, or Coot Bay Ponds at any time.

- No fishing is allowed from the boardwalk at West Lake or at the Flamingo marina during daylight hours.

Lobster and Queen Conch

- The taking and possession of lobster and queen conch is prohibited.

Recreational Crabbing

- Stone crabs, during open state season, and blue crabs may be taken by recreational fishermen using attended gear (star trap, baited line, landing net, etc.).

- Crabbers are limited to five traps.

- Unattended gear, including traps, is prohibited.

Shrimp

- Shrimp may be taken by dip net (not wider than 3 feet/0.9 meter) or cast net for personal use only, not for sale.

Suggested Books and Web Sites

Web Sites

Water's Journey Everglades:
www.theevergladesstory.org
South Florida Water Management District:
www.sfwmd.gov
Everglades National Park:
www.nps.gov/ever/planyourvisit/boating.htm
http://myfwc.com/recreation/boat_index.htm
The Wildlife Foundation of Florida:
www.wildlifefoundationofflorida.com
Audubon of Florida:
www.audubonofflorida.org
ClubKayak.com:
www.clubkayak.com

Books

Grunwald, Michael. *The Swamp* (Simon & Schuster, 2006)

Molloy, Johnny. *A Paddler's Guide to Everglades National Park* (University Press of Florida, 2000).

Molloy, Johnny. *From the Swamp to the Keys* (University Press of Florida, 2003).

Huff, Sandy. *A Paddler's Guide to the Sunshine State* (University Press of Florida, 2001).

Ohr, Tim. *Florida's Fabulous Canoe and Kayak Trail Guide* (World Publications, 2006).

National Audubon Society. *National Audubon Society Field Guide to Florida* (Alfred A. Knopf, Inc., 1998).

About the Author

Loretta Lynn Leda is an avid boater, canoeist, and kayaker who has explored from the Florida Keys and the Everglades up the coast to the outer banks of North Carolina, as far north as Quebec, as far west as Oregon, and as far south as Belize.

She has written for numerous newspapers and magazines and publishes a monthly sports, fitness, health, and adventure magazine in print (*Fit 4 Sports*) and online (www.fit4sports.net). An active member in the Florida Outdoor Writers Association (FOWA), she also serves on the board for the Orange Audubon Society and lives in Winter Garden, Florida.